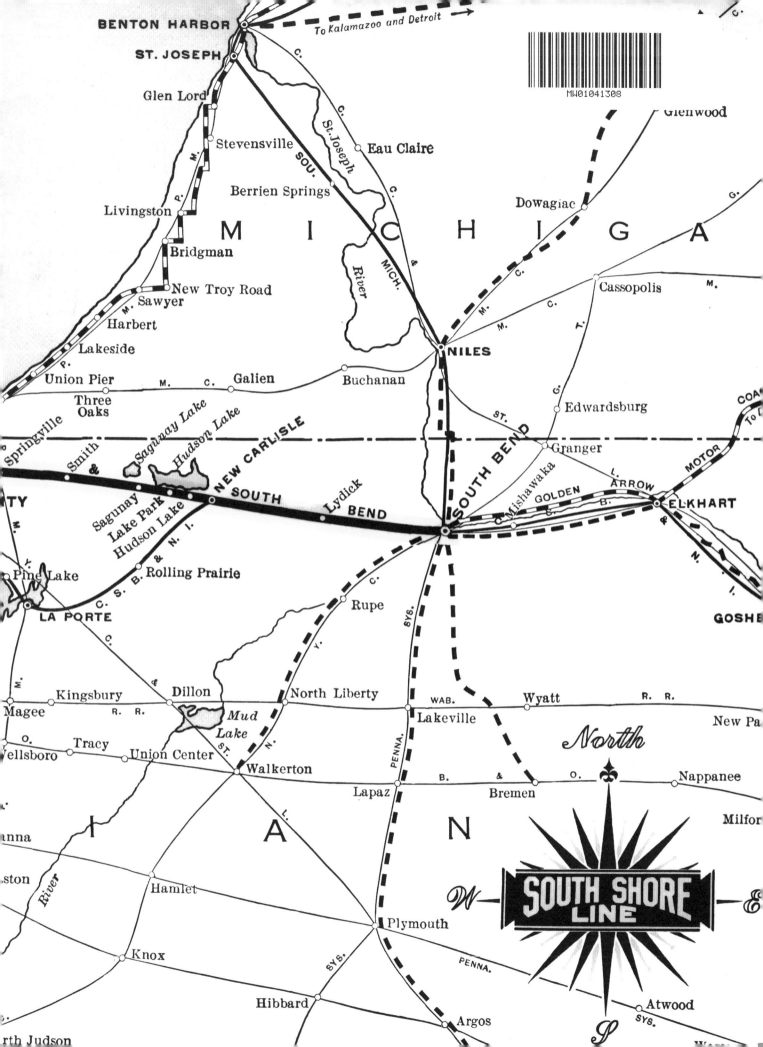

South Shore

The Last Interurban

REVISED SECOND EDITION

William D. Middleton

Indiana University Press

Bloomington and Indianapolis

Title page illustration: **On a hot summer afternoon in 1964 South Bend–Chicago limited train No. 24 roars westward at high speed on South Shore double track near Miller, Indiana. Lengthened and modernized steel cars, the compound catenary and steel overhead bridges of the 1926 *Ideal Section*, automatic block signals, heavy rail and crushed rock ballast are all representative of the modern electric railroad the one-time interurban became. —WILLIAM D. MIDDLETON**

This book is a publication of

Indiana University Press
601 North Morton Street
Bloomington, Indiana 47404-3797 USA

www.indiana.edu/~iupress

Telephone orders 1-800-842-6796
Fax orders 1-812-855-7931
E-mail orders iuporder@indiana.edu

© 1970, 1999 by William D. Middleton
Original edition published in 1970 by Golden West Books, A Division of Pacific Railroad
Publications, Inc., San Marino, California.

Manufactured in China

Library of Congress Cataloging-in-Publication Data

Middleton, William D., date
South Shore : the last interurban / William D. Middleton. — Rev. 2nd ed.
p. cm.
Includes bibliographical references and index.
ISBN 0-253-33533-7 (cl : alk paper)
1. Chicago, South Shore and South Bend Railroad. 2. Street-railroads—Illinois—Chicago—History. I. Title.
TF725.C44M53   1999
388.4'6'097731—dc21   98-55983

1 2 3 4 5   04 03 02 01 00 99

Contents

Despite the arrival of a third generation of rolling stock that reflected main-line railroad standards and dimensions, the South Shore Line manages to retain much of the character of the storied electric interurbans that once passed through almost every corner of the Indiana countryside. Shiny in its newness, Nippon Sharyo–built car 4 headed fast-moving South Bend–Chicago train 8 through rural St. Joseph County near New Carlisle, Indiana, in July 1983. — WILLIAM D. MIDDLETON.

PREFACE TO THE SECOND EDITION

One of the most colorful chapters in the history of transportation in North America was that of the electric interurban railway. Derived from the same technology that produced the electric street railway, the interurbans provided a form of fast, frequent, and inexpensive transportation that helped bridge the gap between the horse-and-buggy era in rural America and the modern age of paved highways and the family automobile. Constructed during scarcely two decades of boundless enthusiasm and almost reckless promotion, the interurban-railway industry had reached its peak by the end of World War I, when nearly 10,000 interurban cars operated over a network of more than 18,000 miles of intercity electric railways and in almost every state of the Union. After a period of prosperity that was almost tragically brief, the interurbans began an abrupt decline, and within another two decades had ceased to represent a significant presence in American transportation.

Unique among interurbans was the South Shore Line. Alone among the hundreds of interurbans that once criss-crossed the Upper Mid-

west, the South Shore survives today, still providing electric transportation over the route it has served since the first decade of the century. If by reason of its very survival the South Shore might be called the most successful of all interurbans, its status has not always been so enviable. Although hailed as a technological triumph at the time it was laid down, the South Shore confounded its promoters with the most disappointing sort of financial performance during the very years when the industry in general was enjoying its greatest prosperity. Perilously close to abandonment by the mid-1920's, the South Shore returned to the forefront of the industry after a dramatic reconstruction program—at the hand of utilities tycoon Samuel Insull—which by the end of the decade had remade it into one of the most technically advanced and financially successful of all interurbans. Undone again by the impact of the Great Depression, the South Shore was plunged into a five-year bankruptcy by 1933, and then slowly struggled back to solvency by the end of the decade. During World War II the South Shore transported the greatest traffic in its history, and in the years that followed won for itself a strong and permanent place in the North American railroad network.

While the South Shore prospered as a freight railroad, by the beginning of the 1970's the railroad's passenger service appeared to have little future. Faced with steadily growing losses from its passenger trains, the railroad sought either to gain public support for the service or to end it. It took a struggle of close to a decade to create the public agency that would support and continue the service. Once again, a massive transformation and modernization would extend the career of the electric trains that had served northern Indiana for so many years.

Far more than any tale of uninterrupted corporate success could ever be, the checkered history of the South Shore Line is a rich and colorful narrative. For those who have known it and for those whose effort and perseverance have made its story one of ultimate success, this volume is presented as a fond look back at the first 90 years of the South Shore story.

I am deeply indebted to the many individuals and institutions whose generous assistance has contributed so greatly to the depth and the variety of the historical and pictorial material included in this volume. In writing of the South Shore's glory years of the 1920's, it was my exceptional good fortune to have had available the first-hand recollections of two men who helped to make that era one of the greatest in the railway's entire history. The late Samuel Insull, Jr. tape-recorded memoirs that provided invaluable insight and background to the story of the Insull acquisition and rebuilding of the railway, while the late R.E. Jamieson, then retired as the South Shore's passenger traffic manager, recalled some of the colorful events that can but seldom be found in conventional reference sources. For a wide variety of assistance with the first edition, special thanks are due Joseph M. Canfield, who interviewed Mr. Jamieson; L.W. Birch of the Ohio Brass Company, Robert W. Gibson of the Electric Railway Historical Society, E.M. Gilroy of Mack Trucks, Inc., Cliff Massoth of the Illinois Central Railroad, R.R. Powers of the General Electric Company, D.B. Seem of White Motor Corporation, and John S. Tris of the Chicago Historical Society, who furnished valued photographs from the files of their respective organizations; the late Freeman Hubbard and the late David P. Morgan, then the editors of *Railroad* and *Trains*, who kindly loaned materials from the files of their respective magazines; William C. Janssen, who located several items of exceptional value; the publisher of the first edition, Donald Duke, whose extensive library and personal collection proved invaluable; and finally James B. McCahey, Jr. and Walter W. Weber, then president and superintendent-transportation, respectively, of the South Shore, who made available a variety of materials from the railroad's official files. For their pictorial contributions I am particularly indebted to the late O.F. Lee and C.E. Hedstrom, whose extensive personal collections were made available; to Eugene Van Dusen, who furnished photographs from the joint collection of M.D. McCarter, W.A. Swartz, Harry Zillmer, and himself, which images bear the credit line "MWEH Collection"; to John Gruber, who provided contemporary photography of exceptional quality; to Alfred E. Barker and David L. Waddington, who contributed some splendid rolling-stock drawings; to artist Gil Reid, who so magnificently captured the drama of the South Shore in watercolor; and to many other individuals and firms, whose contributions are individually credited.

In developing the additional material that brings the South Shore story up to date in this second edition, I had the valued assistance of Albert W. Dudley and R.D. Bunton, who served as South Shore president and director–passenger and administrative services, respectively, during most of the period of C&O ownership; Gerald R. Hanas, general manager of the Northern Indiana Commuter Transportation District; John N. Parsons, NICTD's director, marketing and planning; and Daniel J. Gornstein, NICTD manager, equipment and facilities design. David L. Waddington prepared drawings of the newest generation of South Shore passenger cars. Professor George M. Smerk, director of Indiana University's Institute for Urban Transportation and a long-time member of the NICTD board, provided assistance and support to the new edition that have been much appreciated.

William D. Middleton
Charlottesville, Virginia
May 1998

Typical of the heavy trains that operated under the 6,600 volt alternating current catenary of the Chicago, Lake Shore & South Bend Railway was this six-car extra headed by Niles motor car No. 6, ready to depart from the North Main Street terminal in South Bend.—MWEH COLLECTION

1

THE GREAT ALTERNATING CURRENT LINE

AMONG THE hundreds of interurban railway properties that once laced the Upper Midwest together in a network of almost 9,000 miles of electric lines, the South Shore Line has always been different. When its predecessor company, the Chicago, Lake Shore & South Bend Railway, opened between Hammond and South Bend, Indiana, in 1908, the heavy duty, alternating current line, built to exceptionally high engineering standards, was hailed as a new model for interurban railway construction. Fallen into decline and disrepair by the mid-1920's, the South Shore was rescued from the edge of abandonment by utilities tycoon Samuel Insull, rebuilt into a virtually new railway in a massive reconstruction program that is without parallel in interurban history, and again hailed as a model for the future resurgence of what by this time was a rapidly failing industry.

But the South Shore Line has attained an even greater distinction in more recent years, for the South Shore alone among all electric interurbans has achieved the dual feat of survival as an electrically-operated railroad, still transporting freight and passengers over the original route envisaged by its founders over 60 years ago, while managing to transform itself into an important short line railroad that now constitutes an integral part of the North American railway network.

Though the South Shore's earliest predecessor, the Chicago & Indiana Air Line Railway, was possessed of a grand sounding title, it seemed otherwise to be a very limited venture indeed. Incorporated on December 2, 1901, the Chicago & Indiana was capitalized at a mere $250,000. By September of 1903 the company had completed and opened a 3.4-mile streetcar route between East Chicago and Indiana Harbor, Indiana. Construction of even this modest line was not without difficulty, for the company became involved in a franchise dispute with the older Hammond, Whiting & East Chicago Railway — a dispute that ended with both companies laying competing double

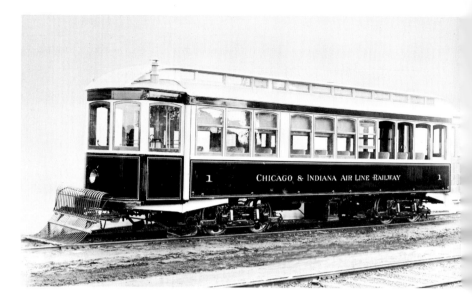

A massive "bed spring" safety fender, designed to scoop up wayward pedestrians, was applied to the front end of the first South Shore car. Two of these suburban cars were built by J. G. Brill in 1903 for the Chicago & Indiana Air Line Railway, the earliest South Shore predecessor. Refitted with larger trucks and alternating current motors in 1908, they continued to serve the railway's East Chicago-Indiana Harbor local line until 1926. — HISTORICAL SOCIETY OF PENNSYLVANIA

track lines down Chicago Street in East Chicago. Two 44-seat suburban cars delivered by Philadelphia carbuilder J. G. Brill in 1903 proved ample to accommodate the line's meager traffic.

But from the very beginning the Chicago & Indiana Air Line had bigger things in mind. The company's original charter called for construction of a railroad extending all the way from South Bend to East Chicago, and even before the initial East Chicago local line had opened in September 1903 the company had secured the necessary franchises for operation through the streets of South Bend, New Carlisle, and Michigan City. A 1904 corporate name change, to the Chicago, Lake Shore & South Bend Railway, defined more exactly the aims of its promoters, which by this time included provision for direct service to Chicago as well.

Although the Lake Michigan south shore region the company proposed to serve was already well endowed with a network of steam railroad trunk lines, the area seemed an unusually promising one for an interurban railway. Well before the end of the 19th century the Calumet District of northern Indiana, which included the communities of Hammond, Whiting, and East Chicago, had begun to emerge as one of the major heavy industrial centers of the Upper Midwest. Consequently, the prospects for a substantial and growing local passenger traffic were exceedingly bright. Previous interurban railway ventures had shown that the

frequent, convenient, low cost service that was possible with electric operation could readily attract a majority of local passenger traffic away from competing steam roads.

In addition to traffic from the Calumet industrial district, studies of potential traffic indicated that the railway could anticipate a substantial volume of travel between South Bend and Michigan City, since there was then no direct means of travel between the two cities. Recreational travel to the Indiana Dunes along the Lake Michigan shore in the vicinity of Michigan City was expected to produce heavy summertime traffic for the electric line.

Across Indiana, Ohio, and New York to the east, a network of interconnecting interurban railways was rapidly nearing completion, and the South Shore Route's promoters visualized their property providing a key link in an unbroken chain of traction lines extending all the way from New York City to Chicago.

Even before the company began any additional construction, a major new industrial project added further to its prospects. Because of its strategic location midway between the coal fields of the South and the iron centers of the Upper Great Lakes, readily accessible by low cost water transportation, the Calumet District by 1901 had become the site of several major steel mills. In 1905 the recently organized United States Steel Corporation began the purchase of some 9,000 acres of Calumet District sand ridges and swamp land several miles east of Indiana Harbor, with a Lake Michigan frontage of seven miles. A year later U. S. Steel began construction on the site of what promised to become one of the largest steel mills in the United States. The building of an entirely new city, named for Judge Elbert H. Gary, chairman of the U. S. Steel board of directors, was an integral part of the project. Population projections for the new city, which was later to become the second largest in Indiana, ranged as high as 100,000 within ten years. Gary lay astride the projected route of the Chicago, Lake Shore & South Bend, and the interurban's promoters lost no time in obtaining franchises and rights-of-way through the new town.

By the fall of 1906 preparations for construction of the new interurban were complete. J. G. White & Company of New York, a prominent electric railway engineering firm, had completed surveys and plans for the entire route between South Bend and Hammond by the end of July. It was anticipated that the vital remaining link required for the provision of direct Chicago service would be built by the Illinois Central Railroad westward from the Indiana-Illinois State Line at Hammond to a connection with IC suburban service at Kensington. By September the South Shore Route's promoters, headed by Cleveland financier James B. Hanna, had increased the company's capitalization to six million dollars, and had obtained the necessary financial backing from a syndicate of leading Cleveland bankers organized by M. H. Wilson, vice president of the Cleveland Trust Company.

A subsidiary company, the South Bend Construction Company, was organized to carry out the actual construction of roadbed, track, and bridges. Contracts for the design and installation of a power plant and the electrical distribution system were awarded to the Cleveland Construction Company.

Construction standards adopted for the line were unusually high. The roadbed was built according to "modern steam railroad practice" and was planned for maximum speeds of 75 m.p.h. For almost its entire length the line was installed on private right-of-way 66 feet or more in width, and a minimum overhead clearance of 17 feet 6 inches was maintained.

The maximum gradient anywhere on the line was two percent, and this only at a single railroad overcrossing. Generally, the gradient

No. 2, one of two original South Shore cars, is seen on Chicago Avenue, East Chicago, around 1908, not long before the two cars were converted to high voltage alternating current operation. — FRED BORCHERT COLLECTION FROM ELECTRIC RAILWAY HISTORICAL SOCIETY (RIGHT) Cleveland promoter and financier James B. Hanna headed the group which organized the Chicago, Lake Shore & South Bend Railway, directed its construction, and became the line's first president. — CLEVELAND PUBLIC LIBRARY

FROM AN ENGINEER'S ALBUM . . .
Between the late autumn of 1906 and the summer of 1908 construction forces under the direction of South Shore Route subsidiary South Bend Construction Company carved a high grade route for the new interurban across the green hills of northwestern Indiana between Hammond and South Bend. An unusually complete photographic record of the work, as well as an excellent portrayal of railroad construction practices of the early 20th century, is provided by these scenes from an album compiled by Wade W. Swasick, a resident engineer for the construction company. (TOP LEFT) Forney type 2-4-4T locomotive No. 64 was one of several South Shore construction engines purchased on the second-hand market. (LEFT) Consolidation type locomotive No. 375 and a steam powered pile driver had just completed work on the Pere Marquette crossing over the South Bend Division of the new Chicago, Lake Shore & South Bend route just east of Michigan City, Indiana, at the time of this photograph.—ALL C. E. HEDSTROM COLLECTION

The raw earth of a just-completed fill shown above, near Hillside on the South Bend Division looked like this in June 1907 before rails were spiked down. (UPPER LEFT) Temporary trestling was nearly complete for a fill under construction just east of Smith on the South Bend Division. (LEFT) The South Shore's own Bucyrus steam shovel No. 465 loads a work train. — ALL C. E. HEDSTROM COLLECTION

A surfeit of rails seems to exist in this view of the still incomplete Chicago, Lake Shore & South Bend Railway taken during 1908 at Chain Lakes, west of South Bend. At right are the tracks of the Lake Shore & Michigan Southern Railway (New York Central), while at the left is the single track line of the rival Northern Indiana Railway.—C. E. HEDSTROM COLLECTION (UPPER RIGHT) The trains would soon be running as the track gang spiked down rails in 11th Street several blocks west of the Michigan City station. (BELOW) Extremely sturdy overhead construction characterized the Chicago, Lake Shore & South Bend's 6,600 volt A.C. installation. This view, taken east of the railway's Michigan City shops, is typical of the pole line and catenary construction utilized on single track portions of the railway.

throughout the line was limited to 0.2 percent or less. With the exception of one six degree curve, the maximum curvature outside of cities was held to three degrees. At various points on the railway tangents of 7, 8 and 14 miles were planned. Even where the line was constructed through city streets — in South Bend, Michigan City, and East Chicago — sharp curvature was avoided. As a later president of the company, Jay Samuel Hartt, was to remark, the line's builder's avoided the common interurban mistake of "wrapping the line around every court house enroute."

Main line track was constructed with 70-pound A.S.C.E. rails laid on 8-foot white oak ties spaced on 24 inch centers and well-ballasted with crushed rock or gravel. An 80-pound Shanghai rail section was used in city streets. Special work was designed to accommodate the standard M.C.B. wheel flange and tread, and standard steam road spring frogs were used throughout. Generally, all crossings with steam railroads were grade-separated. Those in city streets were protected with derailers, and a crossing with the Chicago Outer Belt Line Railroad near East Chicago was protected by an interlocking plant. Initially, the entire line was single track with frequent passing sidings.

Prompted by both a pair of serious accidents in its first year of operation and an order of the Railroad Commission of Indiana, the South Shore in 1913 completed the installation of automatic semaphore block signals on its entire main line. Above is shown the installation at Miller, Indiana. (BELOW) An eastbound train passes the block signals at the end of the Wilson, Indiana, passing siding east of Gary.
—BOTH A. E. BARKER COLLECTION

Highway bridges, culverts, and cattle passes were of reinforced concrete construction, while bridges over other railways were steel structures designed for Cooper's E-50 loading. The only pile trestling used on the entire line was on the approaches to the Calumet River bridge, which were to be replaced later with sand fill and a steel viaduct.

Principal passenger stations for the company were those at South Bend, Michigan City, and Gary. At South Bend the railway constructed a station on Main Street, convenient to the Oliver Hotel, opera house, city hall, county building, and other traction terminals. The Michigan City station was installed in a store building on 11th Street, while a handsome tile-roofed, brick station with car floor level platforms was constructed on Broadway in Gary. Repair shops and the company's general offices were built at East Michigan City.

The most important technical feature of the railway, however, was the choice of a single-phase, alternating current system of power distribution. Almost every system constructed during or before the first big interurban railway boom, which lasted roughly from 1901 to 1904, had adopted the 600 volt direct current system which had become almost universal for street railway systems. At the time, there was no other practical alternative. The low voltage D.C. system had a number of desirable features for light electric railway applications. The system was simple and relatively safe. D.C. motors were fairly light in weight and had particularly good control characteristics. For long distance applications, however, 600 volt D.C. systems had one serious handicap. Because of the greater current required, voltage drop was much more severe than it would have been in a higher voltage system, requiring the installation of heavier feeders and provision of substations at relatively frequent intervals.

Later, the development of equipment for D.C. electrification at 1,200 volts or more would provide a highly satisfactory system for interurban railways. At the time construction of the Chicago, Lake Shore & South Bend was being planned, however, the single-phase alternating current system was being advanced as a superior alternative to 600 volt D.C. electrification.

The principal advantage offered for single-phase A.C. was the great reduction possible in the size of feeders and the required number of substations, which permitted a substantial economy in initial construction costs; some engineers estimated that electrical equipment costs could be reduced by as much as 15 percent. Although motors, controls, transformers, and other equipment required on A.C. motor cars increased their weight by anywhere from 15 to 25 percent over that for comparable D.C. motor equipment, significant reductions in both operating and maintenance costs were also claimed for the single-phase system.

Developed by the Westinghouse Electric & Manufacturing Company, single phase A.C. had first been used in 1904 on the Indianapolis & Cincinnati Traction Company, where a distribution voltage of 3,300 was employed. By 1907, however, Westinghouse was offering a 6,600 volt system. The Chicago, Lake Shore & South Bend's consulting engineers, J. G. White & Company, estimated its adoption would produce a saving of some $240,000 in construction costs, and the decision was made to employ the new Westinghouse system.

Power was supplied to the railway from a single, company-owned power plant at Michigan City, located adjacent to the harbor where an ample water supply was available for boiler feedwater and condenser operation. Six Babcock & Wilcox Stirling boilers, each rated at 500 h.p., supplied 200 p.s.i. superheated steam to three 1,500-k.w. Westinghouse-Parsons steam turbines. Each turbine drove a 1,500 r.p.m. 25-cycle A.C. generator which supplied power at the 6,600 trolley wire voltage.

Adoption of the 6,600 volt single-phase system permitted the railway to distribute power over its entire 76-mile line with only two principal substations located 22 miles east and 31 miles west, respectively, of the Michigan City power plant. Three 1,000 k.w. transformers in the power plant stepped up voltage to 33,000 for transmission to the substations. Three 500 k.w. transformers stepped down current to the 6,600 trolley wire voltage in the Calument substation at East Chicago, while two similar units were installed in the substation at Terre Coupee, two miles east of New Carlisle. Power was also supplied to the trolley wire directly from the power plant.

For reasons of safety, the railway's franchises for operation through the streets in South Bend, Michigan City, and East Chicago required the use of low voltage current. To comply with this requirement the electrical system at these locations, as well as at the Michigan City car shops, was arranged for 700 volt A.C. operation. A total of eight small, low voltage substations was installed in the three cities for this purpose.

The 6,600 volt trolley wire was suspended from a one-half inch steel catenary cable, supported by trolley brackets on poles spaced at 166 feet. The same poles were utilized to carry 33,000 volt transmision lines, telephone, and signal lines. Poles were heavy, 45-foot creosoted Southern pine poles nine inches in diameter at the top. Each was set six feet in the ground and embedded in concrete. Within city streets span wire support was used for the overhead wire in place of trolley bracket supports.

Operation of the railway was by timetable and train order with a single dispatcher in the company headquarters at Michigan City controlling the entire railway. Instead of train order stations, each passing siding or major stop was provided with a telephone booth containing an Egry autographic register for trainmen's use in taking and recording telephone orders. To assist the dispatcher in handling trains by telephone, an unusual Telegraph Signal Company block signal system of the positive selector type was installed. Semaphore block signals at each passing siding could be set at the stop position by the dispatcher. After stopping and receiving any train orders, a conductor could clear the signal on order from the dispatcher and proceed. Because of interference problems from the high tension transmission lines, block signals were frequently set at unintended sidings, resulting in such delays to trains that the entire system was soon abandoned. Similar interference problems also rendered the company's telephone system virtually useless, re-

sulting in enormous bills for long distance calls over regular Bell system telephone lines before the trouble was finally cleared up.

Actual construction work, consisting of grading between South Bend and Michigan City and between Gary and Indiana Harbor, began late in 1906. Work continued steadily through the spring of 1907. One of the first trips made over the "Hanna Line," as it was widely known, was a special run made on June 8, 1907. Organized by the railway's South Bend attorney, F. J. Lewis Meyer, the junket was intended to reassure South Bend city officials who were dubious about the road's progress and reluctant to grant a time extension to the July 1st deadline date for commencement of operations stipulated in the franchise awarded several years previous. Members of the City Council, the Board of Public Works and other city officials, with members of the press and a party of railroad officials led by president J. B. Hanna, were transported by carriage to the city limits, where they boarded a special train for a run over the portion of the road then completed between South Bend and Hudson Lake. The party then continued aboard a Lake Shore & Michigan Southern steam train to La Porte, and thence via interurban to Michigan City, where they viewed progress on "Hanna Line" installations before continuing on to Gary, Hammond, and Chicago. After a lavish banquet the junketing officials were given tickets to "The Man of the Hour," a drama contrasting righteous and corrupt manipulation of railroads. On the following morning the party was taken for a dining car excursion over the Aurora, Elgin & Chicago Railroad, a high speed interurban controlled by some of the same Cleveland financial interests that were backing the CLS&SB, after which they returned to South Bend and promptly voted the needed time extension.

Another problem faced during 1907 by the Chicago, Lake Shore & South Bend was a running battle with the Northern Indiana Railway, known as the "Murdock Line," whose construction crews were racing to construct a line parallel to the South Shore Route westward from South Bend. Fights between track gangs of the rival lines were frequent, and Northern Indiana Railway officials managed to harass the "Hanna Line" with a series of injunctions prohibiting necessary crossings of their lines. The "Murdock Line" was able to open through service between South Bend and Michigan City soon after the CLS&SB began operation the following year but the Northern Indiana line, constructed to lower standards and operating over a longer route via La Porte, was never able to offer serious competition.

With construction of the line nearing completion, the CLS&SB placed an order with the Niles Car & Manufacturing Company of Niles, Ohio, late in 1907 for 24 interurban passenger cars, which were to be built to exceptionally high standards. Delivery of the new equipment began the following March. Constructed of wood, with six-inch steel I-beam underframes, the cars were 57 feet 2 inches in length and weighed over 55 tons fully equipped. Unlike most interurban cars, they were built to a full steam coach width of 10 feet. Couplers and other appliances on the cars were in strict conformance with steam railroad M.C.B. standards. Nine of the cars were arranged as combination passenger, smoking, and baggage cars, while the remaining 15 were fitted out as coaches, with separate passenger and smoking compartments seating a total of 62 passengers. Four of the latter were delivered as trailers, but were converted to motor cars several years later.

The big cars were mounted on Baldwin 90-35 M.C.B. trucks with a 7 foot 6 inch wheelbase and 38-inch steel wheels. Electrical equipment included four Westinghouse No. 148 single-phase motors rated at 125-h.p. each and geared for a 75 m.p.h. maximum speed. Multiple-unit control was provided. A pantograph collector was installed at the center of the car, while a trolley pole was provided at each end for operation on low-voltage sections of the line. In order to avoid electrical damage, roofs of the cars were covered with well grounded 16-ounce sheet copper.

Typical of the heavy wooden cars that constituted the Chicago, Lake Shore & South Bend's initial equipment was coach No. 7, one of an order for 24 cars filled by the Niles Car & Manufacturing Company in 1908. Because of the great weight and complexity of their alternating current electrical equipment, each of the cars weighed 55 tons.—O. F. LEE COLLECTION

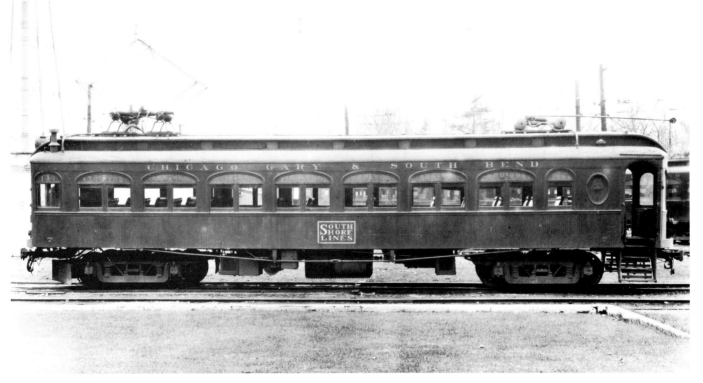

The South Shore's initial fleet of 24 heavy Niles passenger cars was supplemented by 10 of these smaller coach trailers built by G. C. Kuhlman Car Company in 1908. Each of the 28-ton wood cars seated 52 passengers.—CHARLES GOETHE COLLECTION

Interiors of the cars were provided with a full Empire style ceiling, and richly finished in buff and light green, with polished dark mahogany woodwork. Interiors were illuminated by large opalescent dome lights in the ceiling and individual lamps over each seat supported by an artistic bronze bracket. Bronze was liberally used for interior fittings, and the seats were upholstered in black leather. Each car was provided with a lavatory, and was fitted with a Peter Smith hot water heating system. Exteriors were finished in three shades of maroon with silver lettering, an arrangement said to be similar to that of Chicago & Alton limited trains.

A group of ten passenger trailers, built by the G. C. Kuhlman Car Company of Cleveland, Ohio, and a variety of work and service cars, rounded out the company's interurban equipment roster.

For service on its original East Chicago-Indiana Harbor local line and the newer Tolleston Branch in Gary the company re-equipped the two original Brill suburban cars with two 75 h.p. A.C. motors and heavier Baldwin trucks, and ordered two similar cars from the Kuhlman works.

By the summer of 1908 the "Hanna Line" was ready to inaugurate electric operation between South Bend and Michigan City. The first car to make the journey departed from the Michigan City shops at 10:30 a.m. on June 30th in the charge of conductor Peter Dreivlblis and motorman Lew Johnson, accompanied by general manager H. U. Wallace and several other company officials. Owing to an electrical fault near South Bend the inaugural car did not complete the 32-mile trip until 1:35 p.m. Despite the delay, a sizable crowd was on hand to greet the interurban when it finally rolled up to the railway's South Bend terminal opposite the Oliver Hotel on North Main Street. With some 50 fare-paying passengers abroad, the same car departed an hour later on the first westbound trip, which went considerably more smoothly. According to a contemporary newspaper account, the car "fairly flew" and completed the journey to Michigan City in only 1 hour 15 minutes.

Regular scheduled service between the two cities began uneventfully the following morning, with the first revenue run departing from South Bend at 6 a.m. with conductor Taylor and motorman Helm in charge. Initial schedules provided for two hour service throughout the day and into the late evening. The fare between South Bend and Michigan City was 65 cents one way and one dollar for a round trip. Passengers desiring to travel on to Chicago were able to transfer to Lake Michigan steamship services at Michigan City.

In August, with construction nearing completion on the remainder of the line between Michigan City and Hammond, the railway

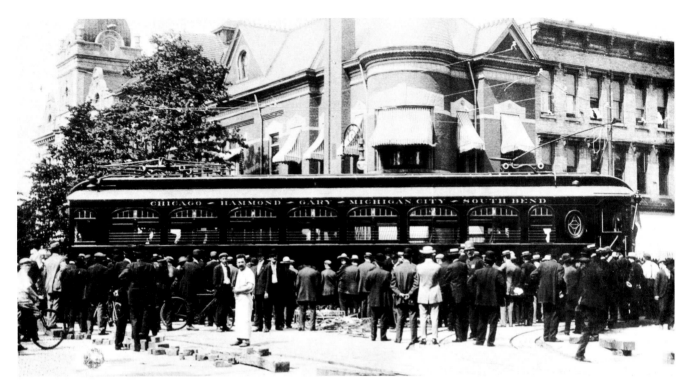

scheduled a "Booster Special," which was to carry a party of prominent Gary business men to South Bend. From South Bend, the party was to continue on to Elkhart and Goshen over the Northern Indiana Railway. The three-car train, under the charge of conductor Dreivlblis and motorman Johnson, proved to be the most ill-favored of special excursions.

Barely out of Gary, all three of the train's pantographs became entangled in the trolley wire on the Baltimore & Ohio Railroad over-crossing at Miller. After a 45-minute delay the journey was resumed, with trolley poles being utilized for the balance of the trip to Michigan City.

At Michigan City the train crew learned that some three miles of trolley wire was down between Tee Lake and Birchim. One of the little steam engines that had been used for construction of the line had been fired up and was ready to carry the train beyond the broken wire. Undaunted, the "Booster Special" pressed on for South Bend. Just out of Michigan City, the train stalled on a grade at the Pere Marquette Railway crossing, and three attempts were required before the little steam engine was able to get the heavy cars over the grade. Further delay was encountered while crew members rode on top of the cars to hold up the deenergized trol-

It was a big day for South Bend when the first Chicago, Lake Shore & South Bend interurban arrived from Michigan City on June 30, 1908. A large crowd was on hand to watch when inaugural car No. 1 was turned on the wye at Main Street and Colfax Avenue, where "some little difficulty" was experienced because the rails in the sharp curve had not been greased, and the car was delayed in getting started on the return trip to Michigan City. Regular service started the following morning.
— MWEH COLLECTION AND SOUTH BEND TRIBUNE

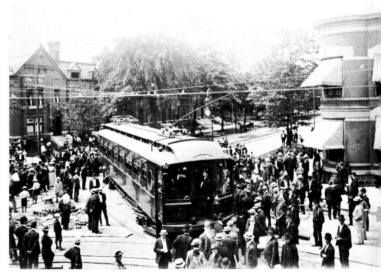

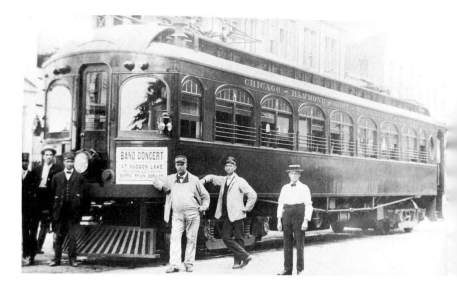

Niles coach No. 3 waited for departure time from the South Shore's North Main Street terminal in South Bend around 1908. The dash sign advertised a summer band concert at Hudson Lake, midway between South Bend and Michigan City, which has remained a popular destination for South Shore excursionists for more than 60 years. (RIGHT) Combination car No. 76, operating as westbound South Bend-Kensington local train No. 14, discharged passengers at Miller station, just east of Gary. —BOTH MWEH COLLECTION (BELOW) For some reason now unknown, Niles combine car No. 70 was missing its pilot at the time of this photo, taken around 1910. — FRED BORCHERT COLLECTION FROM ELECTRIC RAILWAY HISTORICAL SOCIETY

ley wire as the train crawled past the location of the break. By this time the engine had run out of water, and the fire was pulled at Lake Park. Enough steam remained to take the train within a mile of New Carlisle. It had taken nearly six hours to get this far, but according to accounts of the excursion the remainder of the trip to South Bend was made "without further misadventure". The Elkhart and Goshen connection, however, had been missed.

Regular service between South Bend and Hammond began on September 6, 1908, with an initial schedule of ten trains daily in each direction. Passengers desiring to continue to Chicago transferred at Calumet to steam trains of the Lake Shore & Michigan Southern Railway, which terminated at Chicago's La Salle Street Station. The entire 91-mile journey between South Bend and Chicago took some three hours. An all-electric journey to Chicago was also possible by means of a connection with surface car lines at either East Chicago or Hammond.

Meanwhile, work was going ahead on a more permanent solution to the problem of a Chicago connection. Under an agreement with the CLS&SB, the Illinois Central Railroad was constructing a connecting line — the Kensington & Eastern Railroad — between the State Line at Hammond and IC's suburban line at Pullman. Upon its completion, the K&E was leased to the CLS&SB, and the interurbans com-

Typical of the heavy trains operated by the Chicago, Lake Shore & South Bend is this view of westbound train No. 238 running through the Indiana Dunes area. Two of the heavy Niles motor cars, each powered by four 125 h.p. single phase motors, handled four Kuhlman trailers with ease.

Power for the Chicago, Lake Shore & South Bend trains came from the railway's own power plant at Michigan City. Visible in this interior photograph are the 1,500 k.w. Westinghouse-Parsons turbogenerators that supplied the 6,600 volt alternating current.—ELECTRIC RAILWAY JOURNAL FROM LIBRARY OF CONGRESS

menced operating through to Pullman on April 4, 1909. Schedules were closely coordinated with those of IC suburban trains operating to and from the railroad's Van Buren Street and Randolph Street stations in the Chicago Loop. An overhead footbridge at Pullman provided a connection between the South Shore platforms and those of the suburban trains. "This arrangement," stated general manager H. U. Wallace, "I hope will be temporary."

Even before a track connection had been made with the K&E a runaway interurban car had headed west across the State Line in an unusual mishap. Several months previous to completion of the connection a westbound car operated by conductor Rinearson and motorman Kahl experienced difficulty in raising the pantograph at the East Chicago wye. The crew left the car to attempt to raise the pan from the pantograph relay magnets beneath the car, unaware that the controller had stuck on the third or fourth point.

As soon as the pantograph touched the wire the car glided off to the west, moving too rapidly for the crew to climb back aboard. Gathering speed, the runaway interurban raced across one electric line and two different steam railroad crossings in Hammond before running off the end of the track at the State Line, where it

hurtled across Gostlin Street and the tracks of the Indiana Harbor Belt Railroad before coming to rest in soft mud on the Kensington & Eastern side of the State Line. Although the interurban car suffered little damage beyond a lost pantograph, the IHB tracks and interlocking rods were entirely wiped out at the point of the unorthodox crossing.

Knowing that the end of the line was not far away, the car's crew had gamely set out on foot in pursuit of the runaway. Near the State Line they encountered the car's only two passengers walking back toward Hammond. Highly indignant, the two men demanded to know why the car no longer stopped at Hammond.

Despite its high equipment and construction standards, and the optimistic predictions of its developers, the Chicago, Lake Shore & South Bend was anything but an immediate success. Completion of the entire line had taken more than a year longer than originally estimated. Construction costs had exceeded the original $2,500,000 estimate by some two million dollars. The construction company, which had placed the railway in operation even before its completion, had managed to post an operating deficit of almost $52,000 by the time the line was turned over to the railway management on July 1, 1909. By the end of the year a further

operating deficit of almost $80,000 had been accumulated.

Although the railway's charter had contemplated freight as well as passenger traffic, its consulting engineers had concluded that the road was not likely to benefit from freight operations. Consequently, little attention was given in its construction to the location of sidings or provision of other facilities that might benefit freight traffic. An attempt was made early in 1909 to inaugurate regular freight service between South Bend and Hammond, utilizing a combination baggage-passenger car. The service proved unsuccessful, however, and was soon discontinued.

Two serious accidents during its first year of operation did little to improve the South Shore Route's fortunes. On April 12, 1909, westbound train No. 30 overran a meeting point at Clark, just west of Gary, and collided head-on with eastbound train No. 33 near Cavanaugh, injuring 47 persons. Barely two months later, on June 19th, an almost identical accident had even more serious consequences. Overlooking orders to meet train No. 58 at Wilson, the crew of eastbound train No. 59 continued past the meeting point and collided headon with No. 58 at Shadyside, killing 12 and injuring 52. The combined injury and damage claims from

In a view evidently taken only shortly after the railway's opening, a three-car South Shore train was lined up for a broadside publicity photograph that included Niles combine No. 73 and coach No. 6, and Kuhlman coach trailer No. 109.—C. E. HEDSTROM COLLECTION (BELOW) Two tragic accidents marred the South Shore Line's first year of operation. This savage head-on collision at Shadyside, Indiana, on June 19, 1909, was the result of an overlooked meet order, killed 12 and injured 52. It was one of the worst accidents in the railway's entire history.—MWEH COLLECTION

the two accidents totaled over $120,000. Investigation of the latter accident by the Indiana Railroad Commission was highly critical of the railway. Members of the guilty train crew appeared to have been extremely casual about taking train orders, and neither the motorman, who was killed, nor the conductor were believed to have a copy of the order in question after the accident. Conductor Kinney was found to have been discharged previously by the Wabash Railroad for drinking on duty, and may have been drinking before the fatal accident. "To have employed him was the worst railroading we have ever known," said the Commission, "and it may be compared to shooting a gun into a crowd of people."

Having gotten off to what can hardly be termed other than an exceedingly bad start, the Chicago, Lake Shore & South Bend made a valiant effort to improve its performance. In October 1909 management of the company was turned over to the Warren Bicknell Company of Cleveland and Charles N. Wilcoxon, the former general manager of the Cleveland, Southwestern & Columbus Railway, was employed as general manager.

Pleasure and excursion travel were vigorously promoted by the new management. Company advertising featured the bathing beach and amusement park at Michigan City. A special 50 cent round trip excursion fare, for example, drew 2,700 South Bend pleasure seekers

After April 4, 1909, when Chicago, Lake Shore & South Bend trains began running all the way to Pullman over the leased Kensington & Eastern, the Illinois Central's suburban service provided the most convenient connection to the Chicago Loop for South Shore passengers. Typical of the trains that provided the connecting service until IC electrification in 1926 was this four-car suburban run, southbound at 29th Street in Chicago behind a 2-4-4T locomotive. Interior appointments of the Illinois Central equipment were not particulary luxurious.—BOTH ILLINOIS CENTRAL RAILROAD

to Michigan City for the 1910 Labor Day holiday. A company-owned park at Hudson Lake, which offered weekend cottages and picnic facilities, was another popular destination for pleasure travel. Hudson Lake Park picnic specials soon became an important source of additional revenue. One, an 11-car picnic train which transported some 900 employees of the Pullman Company to Hudson Lake in July 1910, was the longest train yet operated by the company and created a sensation as it traveled over the line. Later, such trains became a common sight on the railway.

Although 1910 ended with a net operating deficit of $208,000, work continued on projects to improve the line and its services. The original single track west of Gary had proven inadequate to efficiently carry a scheduled traffic that in 1910 totaled 54 daily trains. A project to double track the railway between Gary and Hammond had been completed in late October 1910, and electrification of a second track all the way to Kensington was completed by December 1911. Two years later the South Shore contracted with the Union Switch & Signal Company to provide semaphore block signals on the entire remaining single track main line between South Bend and Gary.

During 1911 a new interlocking plant was built at Kensington, permitting CLS&SB trains to cross over the Illinois Central main line tracks directly to the suburban platforms, a more convenient arrangement than the overhead footbridge interchange previously in use at Pullman.

An additional source of revenue for the company was developed through the sale of power for commercial purposes from the Michigan City power plant. To keep up with the growing demand a 3,000 k.w., 60 cycle steam turbine and generator, as well as other improvements needed to increase power plant capacity, were installed during 1911.

Whatever the railway's success in promoting excursion travel, the day-to-day traffic of the CLS&SB continued to fall short of original expectations. The lack of through service into the Chicago Loop seemed to be the major deterrent to traffic growth, and in 1912 the company was successful in negotiating an agreement with the Illinois Central that provided for at least a limited through service. Under the terms

After 1912 through coaches, operated on seven trains daily in each direction between Gary and Chicago, provided a more convenient service into Chicago for at least some of South Shore's passengers. In this 1912 view at Gary, eastbound Pullman-South Bend train No. 17 stands in the station at left, while a Gary-Chicago through express is ready to depart at the right.—ELECTRIC RAILWAY JOURNAL FROM LIBRARY OF CONGRESS

Illinois Central suburban locomotive No. 1450 was typical of the motive power that transported the South Shore connections between Randolph Street Station and Kensington. The engine, signed for South Bend by the smoke box, had earlier turned over a through train to South Shore electric power at Kensington when this photograph was taken.—GERALD M. BEST

Several of these secondhand Santa Fe coaches were acquired about 1917 to provide additional equipment for the South Shore-Illinois Central through operation into Chicago.—MWEH COLLECTION

of the agreement, which was placed in effect on June 2, 1912, through coaches were operated between Gary and Randolph Street Station in Chicago on seven daily trains in each direction, connecting closely with limited schedules to and from South Bend. Coaches for the service were provided equally by each company. A South Shore motor car hauled the cars between Gary and Kensington, where a change was made to IC steam power for the run to Randolph Street over the Illinois Central's through tracks. Total running time for the 31-mile journey between Gary and Randolph Street, including a five-minute stop for the motive power change, was 1 hour 15 minutes. The original agreement limited through car operation to Gary, and passengers to and from points east of Gary were still obliged to change cars. Even so, traffic between Chicago and points along the CLS&SB promptly increased by 25 percent. Subsequently, the agreement was modified to permit through car operation as far as Michigan City and, later, all the way to South Bend.

The enthusiasm for single-phase alternating current electrification that had led to its adoption for the Chicago, Lake Shore & South Bend proved to be short-lived. No interurban adopted the A.C. system after 1910, and altogether only some 21 interurban lines in the United States and Canada adopted some form of A.C. electrification. The CLS&SB was one of the few major systems to adopt A.C. distribution, and was the only one to retain it for an extended period of time. Consequently, the railway was the subject of periodic articles in the electric railway trade press discussing its experience with the A.C. system.

There was no questioning the lower original construction costs claimed for the A.C. system, just as there was no questioning that the greater weight and complexity of the A.C. equipment substantially increased the weight of motor cars, and consequently increased operating costs. The South Shore's 55-ton motor cars, for example, weighed a good 10 tons more than typical D.C. motor equipment of comparable size. Most critics of A.C. electrification claimed that it was considerably less reliable, and that maintenance costs were substantially higher. CLS&SB experience, however, failed to substantiate these claims. Except for a period of several years during and immediately following World War I, when maintenance standards fell off, the line's A.C. equipment had an excellent record for reliability. In 1915, for example, the railway was able to boast a five-year passenger train on-time performance record of 95 percent or better. In 1915, too, the company reported equipment maintenance costs of slightly over 2.5 cents per car mile. If this was slightly higher than typical experience for D.C. equipment it was not out of proportion, considering the greater power and capacity of the South Shore equipment.

One of the principal disadvantages of the railway's A.C. installation was the requirement for low voltage operation through city streets in South Bend, Michigan City, and East Chicago, necessitating no less than five stops between South Bend and Hammond for the purpose of switching over a car's electrical equipment and changing between pantograph and trolley pole current collection. Occasionally motormen inadvertently ran through the breaker between 700 and 6,600 volt sections, usually resulting in electrical equipment damage sufficient to disable a car. Moreover, the low voltage system provided insufficient power to get much more than a two-car train out of town; when heavier trains were operated it often became necessary to send someone out to the city limits to temporarily change over the city line to 6,600 volts. Fortunately, the railway was able to discontinue the low voltage operation by 1913, and thereafter the entire line was operated at 6,600 volts.

By far the greatest advantage of the South Shore's A.C. installation was the great power of the Niles motor cars and the exceptional capacity of the electrification system to absorb the unusual traffic demands that were characteristic of the railway. The powerful motor cars were capable of walking off with a six-car train of steam railroad coaches without difficulty, and their power and ruggedness fre-

quently enabled the railway to maintain service under heavy snow conditions that tied up every other railroad in the vicinity. In a 1922 article discussing the railway's experience with A.C. equipment, president and general manager Wilcoxon cited one extraordinary special movement, when the Chicago Geological Society staged a pageant in the Indiana sand dunes near Tremont; within a period of only an hour and a half six trains of 12 cars each and one of 18 cars were dispatched from Kensington without difficulty. At other times, trains of as many as 20 cars were operated.

The great power and capacity of the South Shore's A.C. installation permitted exceptionally high operating speeds as well. A favorite diversion of South Shore motormen was racing the New York Central's crack *Twentieth Century Limited* where the two lines paralleled each other between South Bend and New Carlisle. More often than not, it was claimed, the contest was won by the speedy electric cars.

Limited train schedules of the CLS&SB were easily among the fastest interurban schedules of their time. In 1913, for example, the fastest limited trains were scheduled over the 34 miles between Michigan City and South Bend in only 57 minutes, an average speed of almost 36 m.p.h. While this performance may seem modest today, it was a remarkable one by contemporary standards, particularly in view of the limitations imposed by three intermediate stops and operation through city streets in both South Bend and Michigan City.

In 1924, when *Electric Traction* magazine first compiled a nation-wide interurban speed ranking in what was to be become an annual contest, the South Shore's fastest limiteds were averaging almost 34 m.p.h. for the 76-mile run between Kensington and South Bend despite no less than 26 intermediate stops. On the basis of total elapsed time this performance ranked the railway as the 7th fastest U. S. interurban. On an actual running time basis, however, the CLS&SB was second only to the Chicago, Aurora & Elgin Railroad.

One of the most significant developments in the entire history of the South Shore was the company's inauguration of carload freight ser-

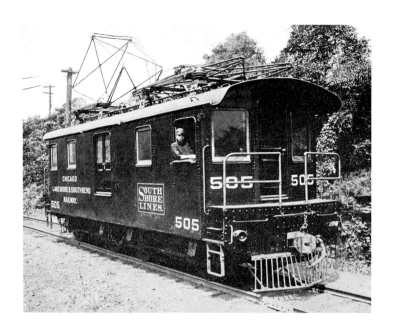

South Shore entered the carload freight business in 1916. Locomotive No. 505 was one of two box cab engines delivered by Baldwin-Westinghouse in September 1916 to handle the traffic. Each of the 72-ton units was powered by four single phase motors delivering a total of 680 h.p. and a maximum tractive effort of 20,800 pounds.—BALDWIN LOCOMOTIVES MAGAZINE

Publicity photograph of Baldwin-Westinghouse locomotive No. 505 operating on the South Shore in 1916.—BALDWIN LOCOMOTIVES MAGAZINE

vice during 1916. Previously, the company had confined itself to package freight, milk, and Wells, Fargo & Company express, which were carried on regular passenger trains. Initially, traffic interchange agreements were established with the Illinois Central and the Elgin, Joliet & Eastern, while negotiations for similar agreements were opened with other connecting steam lines. To accommodate the carload traffic and the planned development of LCL freight service, the railway began the construction of team tracks and freight houses at principal points along its line. To provide adequate motive power for the service, two 72-ton box cab electric locomotives, each capable of handling a train of 30 to 40 cars, were received from Baldwin-Westinghouse during 1916. Twenty all-steel freight cars were purchased at the same time. While revenues from its package freight service had never exceeded a few thousand dollars annually, the South Shore was taking in annual revenues of close to $100,000 from the new carload freight service by 1918.

The enactment of state-wide prohibition in Indiana in 1917 provided the South Shore with a modest source of additional passenger traffic as thirsty Indianans flocked to still-wet Illinois to imbibe or stock up. Gary became a favorite place for enforcement agents to board South Shore trains in search of contraband liquor. Whenever this occurred, there were always a number of pieces of luggage on a train which were suddenly without owners. Extra traffic from this source disappeared as rapidly as it had developed when National Prohibition, which went into effect in January 1920, dried up Illinois too.

The South Shore timetable of April 1918 offered a total of 47 daily trains. All but a few connected at Kensington with Illinois Central suburban trains for the Chicago Loop, and a number carried through cars between Chicago and Gary or South Bend. The centerfold South Shore map delineated connecting interurban routes to Crown Point via the Gary & Southern; to Laporte, Elkhart, and Goshen via the Chicago, South Bend & Northern Indiana; and to Niles and St. Joseph, Michigan, via the Southern Michigan Railway.—PAUL STRINGHAM COLLECTION

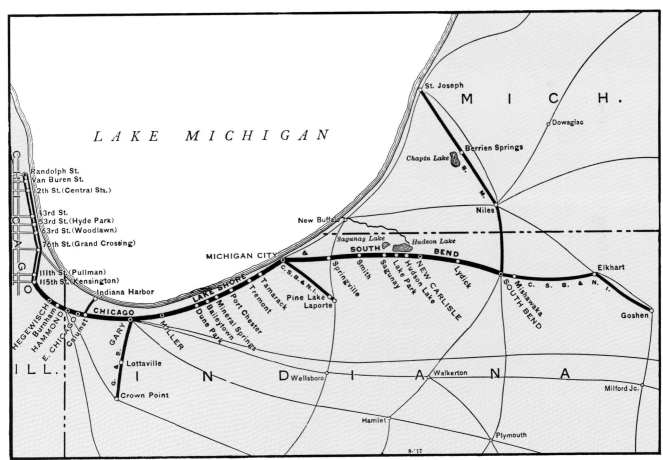

Operation of the South Shore's original local line between East Chicago and Indiana Harbor continued until the end of all alternating current operation in 1926. In the scene above, 48-passenger local car No. 60 is shown at the junction of the local line with the CLS&SB main line in East Chicago.—MWEH COLLECTION (RIGHT) Steel city car No. 64 was built by Kuhlman in 1918 for the South Shore's Indiana Harbor local line. Motors, trucks, and control equipment came from wooden car. No. 60, which had been destroyed by fire.— CHARLES GOETHE COLLECTION At the lower right, No. 64 is seen at East Chicago not long before local operation ended in 1926.—FRED BORCHERT COLLECTION FROM ELECTRIC RAILWAY HISTORICAL SOCIETY

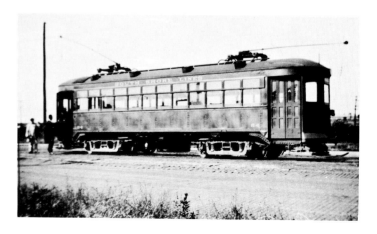

Both during and after World War I the railway's excursion business remained good, requiring some remarkable special movements. On August 11, 1918, for example, the railway handled a Mishawaka Home Guards outing between South Bend and Michigan City, transporting a crowd of 3,000 in two 20-car trains. On July 30, 1922, in what was probably the largest single special movement ever handled by the CLS&SB, nearly 5,000 employees of Chicago's Fair Store were carried to a picnic at Michigan City in six 14-car trains. By 1919 South Bend's University of Notre Dame was beginning its rise to become one of the collegiate football powers of the 1920's under the great Knute Rockne. Any Notre Dame home game in South Bend, or with any of the Chicago area colleges, was the occasion for heavy traffic over the South Shore, both on regular trains and in special movements.

Despite the modest growth of its freight business or the success of its excursion traffic promotion, the South Shore's overall traffic remained exceedingly disappointing. Except for a brief period during World War I, when passenger traffic reached a peak annual volume of over four million in 1917, the railway's daily passenger traffic never reached the volume originally anticipated. In 1921, for example, the South Shore hauled fewer passengers than any other of the seven interurban or suburban electric lines serving the Chicago area. While the seven lines handled an annual total of almost 50 million passengers, and such lines as the North Shore and the Chicago, Aurora & Elgin were carrying totals of almost 12 million and eight million passengers, respectively, the Chicago, Lake Shore & South Bend transported fewer than 2.5 million passengers.

During the decade from 1910 to 1920, when most interurban railways were enjoying their most prosperous period, the South Shore's annual revenues never reached a level of much more than $900,000, and the company's financial performance was among the poorest of any major interurban. In 1914, for example, the CLS&SB was earning less than one percent on its investment.

Wartime conditions brought increased labor and material costs, and the post-war proliferation in automobile ownership and the rapid growth of paved rural highways began to make noticeable inroads on the local passenger business to which the South Shore, in common with most interurbans, looked for the majority of its revenues. In the years immediately following the war the hard-surfaced Lincoln Highway was laid down on a route closely paralleling that of the South Shore all the way from South Bend to Chicago. Although the railway managed to gain some additional freight revenues from the haulage of construction materials for the project, the increased automobile travel and the motor bus and truck competition had a far more damaging and permanent effect on South Shore revenues.

After 1921 the railway's fortunes began a rapid decline. In 1922 the company was scheduling 35 daily trains; a decade before its traffic had required more than 50 daily trains. By 1924 passenger traffic had dropped to some 1.8 million from a 1921 level of over 2.4 million. Freight traffic, which had been at well over 6,000 carloads in 1921, declined to less than 4,000 carloads in 1924. Total revenues fell to less than $800,000. The railway's once-high maintenance standards began to deteriorate. Deferred maintenance accumulated on track and roadbed, and wire breaks in the overhead distribution system and equipment failures became increasingly frequent. The decline was evident in the South Shore's passenger train on-time performance record, which fell from better than 95 percent in 1921 to less than 89 percent in 1923 and less than 92 percent in 1924.

Despite the general prosperity of the 1920's, almost the entire interurban railway industry had been experiencing similar severe declines in traffic and profits ever since the end of World War I. Hundreds of miles of track had already been abandoned, largely by the smaller, weaker lines, but by 1925 even some of the more important systems were beginning to go. Just such a fate seemed to be the only possible end to the South Shore's predicament.

By the beginning of 1925 the South Shore's plight had become desperate. Through the end

31

THE BLIZZARD OF 1918 ... One of the worst snowstorms in South Shore history began on January 11, 1918. During the next several days a phenomenal snowfall and sub-zero temperatures brought activity to a near halt in the communities along the South Shore between Gary and Chicago. Train service was disrupted for a week or more while the railway struggled to dig out from the unprecedented blizzard. At the upper left, South Shore trains still running despite deep drifts on every side. — MWEH COLLECTION (BELOW) The front platform of freight motor No. 506 was heaped high with snow during clearing operations on the Indiana Harbor line just east of the main line junction near Calumet.—C. E. HEDSTROM COLLECTION

The Russell snowplow, several of the passenger cars, and a box motor all appear to be stuck fast in drifts in these scenes photographed at East Chicago in the aftermath of the great storm.— BOTH MWEH COLLECTION

A miscellany of equipment is visible in the view below photographed during snow removal work at East Chicago. — STEPHEN D. MAGUIRE COLLECTION (LOWER RIGHT) Severe winter weather raised havoc with South Shore Line schedules during the blizzard of 1913. Here cars were snowbound in the South Bend terminal. —MWEH COLLECTION

of 1924 the CLS&SB had accumulated a net deficit of over $1.7 million. From an original capital investment totaling over $10 million, the value of the property had depreciated to barely $6 million. After the failure of the railway's original promoters to develop the South Shore into a profitable operation, the Cleveland Trust Company, which had financed the construction, foreclosed their loan and took possession of the South Shore securities. Unable to market the South Shore stock, Cleveland Trust had been sitting with what remained of its investment ever since, and by 1925 was eagerly looking for a way out of the rapidly deteriorating South Shore situation.

By this time a chain of events that would radically alter the course of the South Shore's fortunes was already in motion.

In 1923 Samuel Insull, the Chicago-based public utilities tycoon whose several utilities properties dominated the gas and electric power business in the Chicago area and much of Northern Illinois, moved into the Northern Indiana utilities market through the formation of the Public Service Investment Company. Public Service Investment, which was soon renamed Midland Utilities Company, was formed to place various northwestern Indiana utilities properties already controlled by Insull and those of the United Gas Improvement Company

of Philadelphia under common Insull management, and to carry out a major utilities expansion program throughout Northern Indiana.

In furtherance of his Midland Utilities expansion plans, Insull early in 1924 asked one of his key lieutenants, Britton I. Budd, to look into the Northern Indiana traction situation to see what might be done.

Shortly afterward Budd, accompanied by Samuel Insull, Jr., the tycoon's only son, and several others, set out to survey the two principal Northern Indiana interurban railways. Traveling in a small group so as not to excite any particular comment, the Budd party rode the Illinois Central to Kensington, transferred to the South Shore for the trip to South Bend, and then continued on to Goshen on the Chicago, South Bend & Northern Indiana Railway, returning to Michigan City via the same line and then to Chicago on the South Shore Line.

The position of the CSB&NI, reported Budd, was "hopeless," since the line "began nowhere and ended nowhere." The South Shore, however, although in very bad shape, appeared to represent a worthwhile investment because of its potential for development of both freight and passenger traffic.

Soon afterward Samuel Insull, Jr., acting for Midland Utilities, entered into negotiations with Cleveland Trust leading to Insull acquisi-

The tremendous power of the South Shore's Niles motor cars is illustrated by this view of combine No. 74 with a picnic train made up of six heavy steel Illinois Central coaches at Hudson Lake, Indiana, in the summer of 1926. Although the new Insull management had taken charge the previous year, the new steel cars had not yet been placed in service.—MWEH COLLECTION

Headed by three Niles motor cars, an east-bound limited train paused at the Michigan City shops in 1925. The unusual consist included two leased steam railroad dining cars. Although they had been repainted and refurbished by the new Insull management, the days of the old wooden cars were numbered.
—O. F. LEE COLLECTION

tion of control of the railway. Under the final contract between the two firms a new corporation — the Chicago South Shore & South Bend Railroad — was to be formed. Cleveland Trust Company was to receive bonds in the new company in the amount of their investment. Midland Utilities agreed to advance $4.5 million to rehabilitate the line, for which it was to receive a 60 percent controlling interest in the common stock of the new corporation, while Cleveland Trust received a 40 percent stock interest.

As a preliminary to the reorganization, the Chicago, Lake Shore & South Bend entered receivership on February 28, 1925. This was purely a legal precaution, which effectively prevented anyone with a real or imagined claim against the old company from filing a lawsuit against the new company as soon as new owners came in with new money.

The new Chicago South Shore & South Bend was formally incorporated on June 23, 1925, and scarcely a week later — on June 29th — the bankrupt CLS&SB was sold at public auction in Gary by order of U. S. District Court Judge Thomas W. Slick. The only bid received — $6,474,843 — was that entered by the new CSS&SB. This famous public sale, which has often been interpreted as Samuel Insull's bidding for the property, was actually no more than a part of the legal proceedings that enabled the new corporation to take over the property, and the amount "bid" was actually paid for by the original bondholders with the bonds they already held. As Insull, Jr., observed many years later, "the so-called sale on the court house steps was a mere formality and didn't have anything to do with the main arrangements whatsoever."

A little over two weeks later, on July 15th, Sam Insull took charge, and began to unfold plans for a massive reconstruction of the property that would be without parallel in interurban history, and which within the space of only a few years would completely transform the dilapidated railway into one of the most successful of all interurbans.

Utilities tycoon Samuel Insull provided the hard cash and the management talent that transformed the South Shore Line into the most successful of all interurbans.—SAMUEL INSULL, JR.

2

INSULL'S SUPER-INTERURBAN

I N THE AMERICAN business world of the 1920's Samuel Insull was a man of almost legendary reputation. Born in obscurity in London, England, in 1859, Sam Insull had risen to his prominence in the public utilities industry through a combination of immense energy and exceptional management ability.

At the age of 21 Insull came to the United States as private secretary to inventor Thomas A. Edison. Before Insull was 30 Edison sent him to Schenectady, New York, to manage his new electrical manufacturing plant, which ultimately was to grow into the great General Electric Company. Leaving GE in 1892, Insull set out on his own in the then-infant central station power business, becoming president of the Chicago Edison Company.

During the next several decades the Insull-managed company, which later became the giant Commonwealth Edison Company, pioneered much of the technology and the business methods which spurred the extraordinary growth of the electric power industry early in

the 20th century, and became the cornerstone of a mammoth Insull-controlled public utilities empire that by 1930 was worth somewhere between two and three billion dollars; generated a tenth of the nation's electricity; and provided electric, gas, and transportation service to some 5,000 communities in 32 states.

Although his efforts had been largely in the public utilities field, Samuel Insull was by no means a newcomer to the electric railway industry when his Midland Utilities Company acquired control of the South Shore Line in 1925. Indeed, Insull's interest in electric railways dated as far back as the early 1880's, when he had participated in some of Thomas Edison's pioneering experiments in railroad electrification, and in later years he had come to believe that electric transportation would ultimately supplant all other means of mass transportation.

Beginning in 1914, when the Chicago elevated system was unified under his control, Insull began acquiring widespread financial or

The tycoon's son, Samuel Insull, Jr. shown on the left, was a key figure in the South Shore transformation. Then only 25 years old and a vice president of Insull's Midland Utilities, "Junior" Insull negotiated the acquisition of the railroad by Midland and then directed its reconstruction as a South Shore vice president.—SAMUEL INSULL, JR. At the right, trusted Insull lieutenant Britton I. Budd, who headed both the Chicago "L" system and the North Shore Line for Insull, was also the reorganized South Shore's president, and brought a tremendous depth of experience to the railroad's reconstruction.—CHICAGO HISTORICAL SOCIETY

management control of electric railway properties. By the time he assumed control of the South Shore, the Insull traction empire included an almost unbroken chain of interurban properties extending from Milwaukee to Louisville, and the electric railway trade press was giving serious attention to rumors that a single giant Insull interurban system was in the making.

Intriguing as the prospects of through interurban operation over such a system might have been, the Insull interest in the South Shore Line stemmed from more realistic considerations. Despite the dismal financial performance of the predecessor Chicago, Lake Shore & South Bend, the region served by the South Shore Line remained one of exceptionally great promise for an interurban railway. The South Shore Line provided a direct link between Chicago and several of the largest cities in Indiana, and between 1907 and 1925 the population in the area directly tributary to the railway had more than doubled, from 175,000 to 390,000. Industrial development in the Calumet District served by the South Shore had continued

unabated since the beginning of the century. Already familiar with the great potential of the northwestern Indiana area through the gas and electric power operations of its utilities subsidiaries, Insull's Midland Utilities Company held an enthusiastic view of future prospects for the South Shore Line.

During the several years immediately previous, an Insull management had capitalized on an almost parallel situation, transforming the bankrupt North Shore Line into one of the finest — and most profitable — properties in the entire interurban railway industry. Sam Insull was confident that the same formula could be successfully applied to the South Shore Line.

Reorganization of the South Shore under Insull management brought a formidable array of management talent to the line. Insull himself was elected chairman of the board. Britton I. Budd, who had been picked by Insull to head Chicago's consolidated "L" system in 1914 and who had directed the North Shore's reconstruction as the line's president following its reorganization in 1916, was elected president of the South Shore. The utilities tycoon's son,

Samuel Insull, Jr., who was a vice president of Midland Utilities and had carried out the negotiations that resulted in Insull control of the South Shore, was elected a vice president and directly supervised the reconstruction of the South Shore. Two remaining vice presidents of the new company, Bernard J. Fallon and Charles E. Thompson, were both officers of the North Shore Line. Charles H. Jones, formerly electrical engineer for both the North Shore Line and the Chicago Rapid Transit, was appointed general manager of the South Shore soon afterward.

With an announced objective of developing a standard of freight and passenger service that would place the South Shore "above competition," the new management immediately initiated a massive reconstruction program for the deteriorated property. Within two months 400 to 500 men were at work on rehabilitation of the railway, and by December 1st the labor force reached a peak of more than 900 men. By the end of the year well over a half million dollars had been expended on the reconstruction work.

During the first few months efforts were largely concentrated on the rebuilding of the railway's track and roadbed. By October a total of 13 track gangs were at work. The entire line between Kensington and South Bend was resurfaced, requiring a total of 300 cars of cinder ballast by the end of the year. Close to 40,000 new creosoted ties were placed, and 11,-000 pairs of heavier angle bars were installed throughout the main line. Between Kensington and Hammond some ten miles of the railway's most heavily traveled double track line was graded, reballasted with crushed rock, and relaid with 100 lb. rail in place of the original 70 or 80 lb. rail. Work was started on a program to lengthen and double-end sidings and to equip them with high speed turnouts, in order to allow the operation of longer freight trains and to permit high speed meets.

Throughout the length of the line the roadbed was widened and drainage ditches improved. Highway crossings were cleared of trees and underbrush which obscured vision, and the entire line was cleared of weeds and other growth. Several new bridges were installed, and all steel structures and bridges were cleaned and painted. Telephone lines were replaced, and the railway's entire block signal system was rebuilt.

Indicative of the advanced state of deterioration of the latter system is a recollection of Samuel Insull, Jr., of a pre-rehabilitation trip over the line. On one section of the line, he recalled, five out of seven block signals were being run on order,or disregarded, by train crews because they were out of service.

Freight stations and platforms were enlarged, and painted in the railway's new standard orange and mahogany color scheme. A new passenger station was opened at La Salle and Michigan streets in South Bend. The stations at Gary and Tremont were rebuilt, and that at Michigan City was remodeled and painted. A standard design was developed for the rebuilding of shelters at all local stops.

Before the end of the year the South Shore had placed orders totaling well over a million dollars with the Pullman Car & Manufacturing Corporation for 25 new steel passenger coaches, two dining cars, and two parlor-observation cars. In anticipation of a greatly increased freight traffic, four new 80-ton freight locomotives were placed on order from Baldwin-Westinghouse at a cost of almost a quarter million dollars.

Without waiting for delivery of its new passenger cars, the South Shore set out to improve passenger service with its existing equipment. Interiors of the original Niles and Kuhlman cars were refurbished, and the cars were repainted in the new orange and mahogany colors. Greatly expanded schedules were placed in effect; by the end of 1925 the company was operating 28 more daily trains than a year previous. Passenger revenues showed an almost immediate increase.

Although the initiation of through coach service over the Illinois Central to Chicago in 1912 had somewhat improved the railway's traffic volume to and from Chicago, the delays incurred in changing motive power and the limited number of through trips had remained a barrier to development of the full traffic po-

A train of the South Shore's hand-some new steel cars, operating as South Bend-Chicago limited train No. 14, was posed for this pub-licity photograph on the newly-completed *Ideal Section* near Mil-ler in the summer of 1926. — WILLIAM J. CLOUSER COLLECTION

As part of the Insull reconstruction program for the South Shore's power system, a completely new *Ideal Section* of overhead construction was installed on a mile of double track near Miller, Indiana, as a prototype for eventual complete replacement of the entire overhead system. Steel overhead bridges spaced at 300 feet supported a compound catenary system.—OHIO BRASS COMPANY

Stations were rebuilt or replaced at a number of South Shore points under the Insull program. This new station built at Lake Shore, Indiana, just west of Michigan City, was constructed to the same handsome "Insull Spanish" design employed for stations on the new Skokie Valley Route of the Insull-controlled North Shore Line.—WILLIAM D. MIDDLETON

tential. One of the principal considerations that had affected the Insull decision to acquire and rebuild the South Shore Line was the opportunity afforded by the impending electrification of Illinois Central's suburban lines to finally overcome this handicap.

Operating as it did along the Chicago lake front, the IC service had always been the target for smoke abatement criticism. In 1912 the City of Chicago had finally forced the issue with an electrification ordinance which required electrification of IC's suburban service by 1927. By 1925 IC was well along with a $50 million terminal improvement program that included not only electrification, but substantial right-of-way improvements as well. Opening of the electric service was planned for the summer of 1926.

In addition to the close ties that had historically existed between the South Shore and the Illinois Central, the Insull interests also had a close relationship with IC at this time. Insull's Commonwealth Edison represented IC's largest coal shipper, and the IC in turn, with its new electrification, represented one of Commonwealth Edison's largest power customers. Even before assuming control of the South Shore the Insull management negotiated a contract with IC that granted South Shore trackage rights for through operation of all trains directly into IC's Randolph Street Station.

Because the Illinois Central electrification employed a 1,500 volt direct current system, through operation of South Shore trains required not only entirely new motor equipment, but the complete replacement of the South Shore's original 6,600 volt A.C. system.

By the end of 1925 the South Shore had begun work on a complete renovation of its overhead distribution system and installation of the new equipment required for D.C. operation. The entire original catenary trolley wire system was replaced, utilizing only the original wood poles, which were found to be in excellent condition. Between Kensington and Hammond new steel supporting trusses for the overhead system were installed on the original poles. Near Miller, Indiana, an "ideal" section of new overhead system was installed on a mile

South Shore began receiving its initial order for 25 new steel passenger cars from the Pullman Car & Manufacturing Company in June 1926. No. 100 was one of ten combination baggage-passenger cars weighing 60 tons and seating 44 passengers.—WILLIAM J. CLOUSER COLLECTION (RIGHT) Substations for the South Shore's new 1,500 volt D.C. power system were constructed by the Insull-controlled Northern Indiana Public Service Company. This was the Grandview substation located at South Bend.—JERRY MARLETTE COLLECTION

of double track line as a prototype for eventual replacement of the entire overhead supporting system. Steel catenary bridges, virtually identical to those used on the North Shore Line's new Skokie Valley Route, were installed at 300 foot spacings, supporting a three-wire catenary system.

To supply the D.C. power, the Northern Indiana Public Service Company, another Midland Utilities subsidiary, began the installation of the necessary feeders and the construction of eight new substations, at Hammond, Gary, Ogden Dunes, Tremont, Michigan City, Tee Lake, New Carlisle and South Bend. Five were of 1,500 k.w. capacity while the remainder were 750 k.w. stations. Among the advanced features of the electrical installation were the provision in four of the new substations of a new type of

At the height of the Insull era South Shore's mid-afternoon South Bend-Chicago parlor car train No. 22, the *Randolph Limited*, loads passengers at Michigan City in the summer of 1927. Both the handsome station and the train's all-steel, Pullman-built equipment were brand new.—COURTESY OF TRAINS MAGAZINE (RIGHT) Coach No. 12 was one of several under the 1926 order equipped with a Pullman type enclosed smoking compartment at one end. Although originally quipped with a pantograph at one end and a trolley pole at the other, the car had been fitted with pantographs at both ends by the time of this photograph.—DONALD DUKE COLLECTION

automatic mercury-arc rectifier, and the use of a carrier current type of supervisory control which permitted centralized control of power supply for the entire railway. Both of these features represented the first such installations on any U. S. railroad.

Deliveries of the new Pullman motor cars began in June 1926. Constructed entirely of steel, the new cars were 60 feet in length, 10 feet 6 inches wide, and weighed 60 tons, representing some of the heaviest cars of their length ever built. Each car was equipped with four 200 h.p. Westinghouse No. 567-C motors, and was mounted on seven foot wheelbase Baldwin type 84-60 AA high speed, heavy duty trucks. The cars were fitted with Westinghouse HBF electro-pneumatic multiple unit control, and were provided with both a pantograph and a trolley pole for current collection.

Ten of the cars were arranged as combination baggage-passenger cars, seating 44 passengers, while the remainder were full coaches, seating 56 passengers. All 25 were provided with separate smoking compartments and two toilet compartments. The cars were equipped with standard steam railroad type vestibules and diaphragms to provide a fully enclosed passage between cars, the first interurban equipment ever so equipped.

Interiors of the cars were finished in rich brown mahogany woodwork, with light cream ceilings and battleship linoleum flooring. Seats were upholstered in deeply cushioned green mohair velvet, or with Pantasote in smoking compartments. Interior trimmings were of statuary bronze, and electric fans and large dome lights were installed. Thermostatically controlled dual electric and hot water heating systems were installed. The electric heaters were sufficient for normal heating requirements, with the hot water system being placed in operation only in extremely cold weather.

Following delivery of a portion of the new steel equipment, the overhead system between South Bend and Michigan City was cut over to 1,500 volt D.C. and the new cars placed in service on July 13, 1926. At the same time three of the new D.C.-equipped Baldwin-Westinghouse freight locomotives were placed in service east of Michigan City. A.C. operation with the old equipment continued west of Michigan City, with trailers operating clear through. D.C. operation was extended to Gary a week later, and the entire line was cut over to D.C. on July 28th. For a short time, pending completion of the IC electrification, the South Shore's new steel cars were hauled to Randolph Street behind steam locomotives. Finally, on August 29, electric operation over the IC line was initiated, and for the first time in its history the South Shore was able to offer a full, direct passenger service to the heart of Chicago. New

Photograph taken on the *Ideal Section* showing a pair of old Chicago, Lake Shore & South Bend semaphore signals which were thoroughly rehabilitated by the Insull management as an interim measure, and then completely replaced by a color light block signal system a few years later.—O. F. LEE COLLECTION

schedules provided for the operation of 56 daily trains, including 31 limited trains. Hourly limited train service was available between Chicago and South Bend throughout the day, and running time between the two terminals was cut by 20 minutes.

In just the first year of Insull management the South Shore Line had invested almost $2.8 million in rehabilitation and improvements to the property and for new equipment, while Northern Indiana Public Service had spent another $857,000 for the installations necessary to convert the railway to D.C. operation. The results of the South Shore's massive reconstruction were immediate and dramatic.

Passenger revenues began an abrupt increase immediately following the installation of through service into Chicago, and freight revenues continued to grow at a steady rate. For the first time in the railway's history, South Shore's annual operating revenues exceeded a million dollars in 1926. Passenger revenues of over $750,000 represented a 25 percent increase over the preceeding year, and freight revenues were up by over 30 percent.

To accommodate the rapid increase in passenger traffic, an order for 20 additional cars was placed with Pullman in January 1927 for delivery the following summer. Ten were equipped as motor cars and ten as trailers. Except for an increase in length to 61 feet, the new cars were mechanically almost identical to the original order. Interior accommodations, however, were substantially improved. Instead of the green plush "walkover" seats installed in the previous equipment, the new cars were fitted with rotating bucket seats upholstered in gray Byzantine plush. In place of the customary smoking section, the cars were provided with an enclosed Pullman type smoking compartment furnished with facing leather covered seats for eight passengers. An aisle passing around the compartment made it unnecessary for passengers entering or leaving the car to pass through the smoking compartment.

Interior appointments of the ten trailers delivered under the 1927 equipment order. The improvements over the South Shore's initial new equipment order including rotating bucket seats, upholstered in Byzantine plush, replacing "walkover" seats of the earlier cars.—DONALD DUKE COLLECTION (BELOW) Three of these 85-ton General Electric locomotives, designed for operation on any of the three Chicago-area Insull interurbans, were received by South Shore in 1930.—MWEH COLLECTION

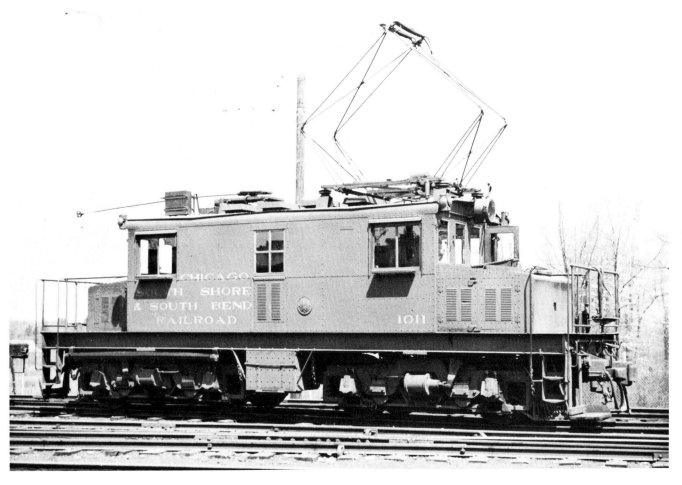

Two 53-ton switching locomotives were ordered from Baldwin-Westinghouse at the same time to provide additional motive power for the South Shore's steadily growing freight traffic. Four additional 80-ton locomotives were ordered later in the year for delivery in 1928.

Even before delivery of its new luxury equipment, the South Shore had experimented with the use of rented steam railroad dining cars, with encouraging results. Late in January 1927 the Pullman works delivered the South Shore's own dining and parlor-observation equipment, which represented an investment of almost $200,000 in deluxe passenger service.

Except for their shorter 64-foot length, the four new cars were constructed to typical steam railroad Pullman car dimensions and standards. Weighing almost 57 tons, probably the heaviest non-motored equipment ever operated in interurban service, the cars were mounted on steam railroad type Commonwealth six-wheel trucks, the only equipment of this type ever placed in regular interurban railway service in North America.

The two parlor cars were arranged with a completely enclosed observation solarium and parlor compartment at each end of the car, permitting operation in either direction without turning the cars. The center portion of the car was given over to a women's retiring room outfitted with a small boudoir table and full length mirror, a men's smoking room, toilets, and a small buffet kitchen for light refreshment service. Total seating capacity was 24.

Parlor car passengers were seated in individual arm chairs upholstered in mohair velvet, and a built-in writing desk and magazine table were provided in each parlor compartment. Interiors were finished with walnut woodwork and floors were covered with deep plush carpets. Interior fittings included bronze parcel racks, electric fans, and both overhead dome lighting fixtures and bronze side fixtures.

The two dining cars were arranged in the conventional steam railroad manner, with seating capacity for 24 passengers. A green, decorated enamel finish was provided in the dining room, which was also fitted with plush carpeting. The cars were outfitted with handsome tables and chairs and fine linens, china, and silverware. The kitchens were laid out with fast service in mind, in order that short haul passen-

Parlor - Observation and Dining Car Service

Top, left—An atmosphere of restful dignity and comfort pervades the main parlor compartments of the new cars.
Top, right—Interior of one of the new dining cars at "first" call for luncheon.

Below, left—A quiet, cozy corner for writing in one of the parlor-observation cars.
Below, right—Luxury and refinement is suggested in the handsome furnishings of the parlor-observation cars.
Below, center—Beautifully appointed ladies' lounge in one of the parlor-observation cars.

Typical Dining Car Menu, Service a la Carte

SOUP		Strawberry or Peach Preserve	30
Mock Turtle in Tureen	30	Orange Marmalade	30
Consommé in Cup	20	Sliced Orange	40
FISH		Preserved Figs in Cream	
Boiled Whitefish, Potatoes	75	Other Fruits in Season	25
CHOPS AND STEAKS		Ice Cream, Wafers	25
Grilled Lamb Chops (3)	80	Pie	15
Special South Shore Steak	1.25	American Cheese, Crackers	15
Ham and Eggs	65	Roquefort Cheese, Crackers	15
Half Milk-Fed Spring Chicken	90	BEVERAGES	
Special South Shore Omelette	65	Coffee, Pot	15	Tea, Pot	15
Steamed Poached Egg and Bacon on Toast	65	Cocoa, Pot	15	Postum	15
VEGETABLES		Individual Bottle, Milk	15
French Fried Potatoes	25		
Stewed Tomatoes	20	Peas	20	Assorted Bread or Hot Rolls, and Butter	15

SOUTH SHORE LINE parlor-observation and dining cars are of heavy, all-steel construction and have been designed to afford utmost ease and luxury in riding. Large, roomy, soft-cushioned chairs, luxurious lounging and smoking rooms and airy, spacious observation platforms invite restful relaxation to parlor car travelers. Buffet luncheons are served on each car.

In the new dining cars, provision is made for serving 24 persons at one time. Meals are prepared in extra-large, immaculate kitchens and served a la carte by experienced and attentive waiters. The cheerful and attractive furnishing of the cars create an environment like that of one's favorite club or hotel. (See page 15 for time schedules.)

INTERURBAN DE LUXE . . . Following delivery of its new heavy steel parlor and dining car equipment from the Pullman works early in 1927, the South Shore inaugurated a luxury service on five limited trains in each direction between South Bend and Chicago that was unexcelled on any interurban. On the opposite page, the westbound *Illinois Limited* in 1929, offering both dining and parlor car service, departing from South Bend at noon.—O. F. LEE COLLECTION (LEFT) Typical menu of the 1927 era offered steak for only $1.25. The menu was included on the inside page of the South Shore's public timetable.—DONALD DUKE COLLECTION

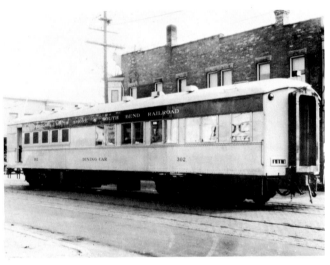

Except for their shorter length, the South Shore's new dining cars, shown above, were virtually indistinguishable from steam railroad equipment.—O. F. LEE COLLECTION (UPPER RIGHT) Interior appointments were said to create an environment "like that of one's favorite club or hotel". (RIGHT) Plush carpeting, chairs upholstered in mohair velvet, and walnut panelling provided South Shore parlor cars with what was described as "an atmosphere of restful dignity and comfort", and a standard of luxury that was equal to the finest contemporary steam railroad equipment.—BOTH GEORGE KRAMBLES COLLECTION

gers would have time to finish their meals.

Arrival of the new equipment was the occasion for an intensive South Shore publicity campaign. On February 10, more than 125 newspaper men, city officials, and other dignitaries from principal South Shore cities were guests of the company on an official inspection tour in the new cars. President Britton I. Budd headed the delegation of company officers that escorted the guests. A few days later the four cars began a six-day exhibition tour of principal on-line cities, during which more than 7,000 persons visited the new equipment.

Regular deluxe limited name train service between Chicago and South Bend began on February 20th, with three dining car and two parlor car trains operating in each direction on 2 hour 30 minute schedules.

Eastbound dining car trains, which operated at breakfast, luncheon, and dinner hours were named the *Notre Dame*, *Indiana*, and *St. Joe Valley* limiteds, while their westbound coun-

The installation of South Shore parlor and dining car service was announced through an intensive publicity campaign. This advertisement, which appeared in South Bend newspapers, was typical of the publicity that preceded the new service. — WAYNE C. OLSEN COLLECTION

terparts were the *Ft. Dearborn, Illinois,* and *Garden City* limiteds. Eastbound forenoon and afternoon parlor-observation trains were the *Duneland* and *Marquette* limiteds, while their South Bend-Chicago opposites were the *Grant Park* and *Randolph* limiteds.

Parlor car seats were available upon payment of a modest 50 cent charge. A la carte dining car menus offered such items as a "Special South Shore Steak" for $1.25, or a half milk-fed spring chicken for only 90 cents. The dining cars were operated by the South Shore's own commissary, which went to great lengths to assure a high standard of service. In 1928, for example, the railroad purchased 15 prize-winning yearling Hereford steers to be used in serving choice cuts on its dining cars during the Christmas season.

The installation of luxury equipment, as well as such new schedules as the *Chicago Theatre Limited,* which offered fast evening service from Gary tailored to Chicago theater hours, contributed to the increasing popularity of the South Shore's passenger services. Effective with the summer 1927 timetables South Shore in-

creased its schedule to provide 72 daily trains, including 40 limited trains operating over the entire distance between Chicago and South Bend. The South Shore, said *Electric Railway Journal,* "has dealt a smashing blow to competition."

The growth of the railway's passenger traffic was phenomenal. During the first six months of 1927 the South Shore's passenger revenues reached a level of more than double those of the corresponding period only a year before.

In promoting the South Shore's vastly improved passenger service, the railway's Insull management team applied many of the same methods that had proven so successful in the rebuilding of the neighboring North Shore Line.

Soon after the Insull management took charge in 1925, the South Shore entered the bus business, as much to forestall competition as to develop valuable feeders to its rail services. Initially, the railway's bus subsidiary — Shore Line Motor Coach Company — operated a service between Michigan City and St. Joseph and Benton Harbor, Michigan. Bus schedules were

An order for 20 new coaches delivered by Pullman in 1927 was divided equally between motor and trailer cars. Except for a one foot increase in length, the new cars were mechanically and electrically virtually identical to the initial South Shore equipment order delivered a year previous. Car No. 201 was one of ten trailer cars, while No. 21 was one of the ten motor passenger cars. — BOTH CHARLES GOETHE COLLECTION (BELOW) Floor plan for the new diners reveal the exceptionally large kitchen, which permitted the South Shore to offer extra fast service for the benefit of short haul riders.

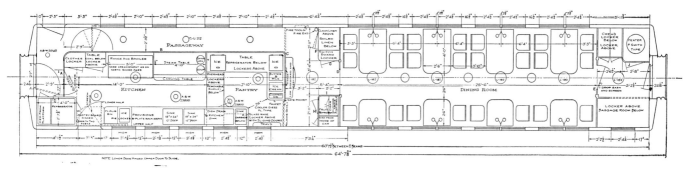

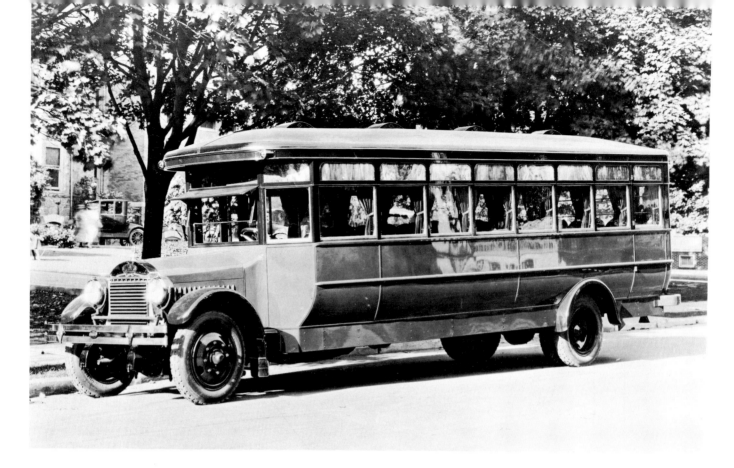

Soon after the new Insull management took charge, the South Shore began developing an extensive bus subsidiary as a feeder to its interurban lines. These three stock illustrations are typical of the Mack Model AB buses delivered to the South Shore bus subsidiary — Shore Line Motor Coach Company — in 1927. Nickel plated radiators, colored "art glass" upper window sash, and leather upholstered wicker seats represented the last word in 1927 motor coach style.—ALL MACK TRUCKS, INC.

closely coordinated with those of the railway, and Shore Line coaches used the South Shore terminal in Michigan City. Within the next year Shore Line Motor Coach extended its service to Holland, Muskegon and Grand Rapids, Michigan. Routes were acquired paralleling the South Shore between Chicago, Michigan City and South Bend. Tickets were good on either buses or trains, but passengers were reminded that the train saved an hour or more. Still other routes were acquired that provided service to points in Illinois and northwestern Indiana, connecting with South Shore trains at Hammond, East Chicago, and Gary. By the end of 1926 Shore Line Motor Coach was operating a total of 26 routes in Illinois, northern Indiana, and southern Michigan. The company's equipment included the newest type Mack coaches, and for its long distance runs into Michigan, Shore Line purchased the latest A.C.F. "parlor observation coaches," which featured a raised rear section remarkably similar to the Greyhound "Super Scenicruiser" of 30 years later.

Blue and gold White Model 54 coaches, specially fitted with overstuffed air-cushioned chairs, curtained windows, toilet and wash room facilities, and a rear smoking and observation compartment, were purchased for the deluxe *Golden Arrow* service between Chicago and Detroit, operated jointly by the South Shore and its bus subsidiary, Shore Line Motor Coach. One-way fare was $7.50 and advance reservations were required.—WHITE MOTOR CORPORATION

In July 1927 the South Shore and Shore Line Motor Coach made a remarkable entry into the long haul passenger trade with the jointly operated *Golden Arrow* service, which ran once daily in each direction between Chicago and Detroit. Eastbound *Golden Arrow* passengers departed from Chicago on the noon dining car train *Indiana Limited* and transfered at South Bend to a non-stop motor coach which made an early evening arrival in Detroit. A similar westbound schedule connected at South Bend with the evening dining car train *Garden City Limited*. The eight and a half hour *Golden Arrow* schedule was said to be fully three hours faster than any other bus service, and nearly as fast as express trains on competing steam railroads.

Golden Arrow equipment represented the very last word in 1927 motor coach luxury. The two 25-passenger White model 54 parlor observation coaches procured for the service were provided with inside baggage compartments, toilet and wash room facilities, and a rear smoking and observation compartment. Passengers

Golden Arrow coaches connected with South Shore limited trains at South Bend. Eastbound passengers left Chicago on the noon dining car train *Indiana Limited*, while the westbound run connected with the evening dining car train *Garden City Limited*. (BELOW) The interior view shows a similar but somewhat less luxurious version of the White Model 54 coach.—ALL WHITE MOTOR CORPORATION

were seated in individual bucket type seats up-holstered in blue leather. The coaches were painted blue inside and out, with gold lettering and striping on the exterior. In imitation of steam railroad observation cars, rear ends of the coaches were fitted with a dummy observation platform railing, scalloped awning, and a drumhead sign.

Travel Luxury on the Highways proclaimed Shore Line Motor Coach advertisements announcing the inauguration of the new Chicago to Detroit motor coach service known as *The Golden Arrow.* — ELECTRIC TRACTION MAGAZINE (**BELOW**) One of the new *Golden Arrow* coaches making a train connection at South Bend. It appears that trip must have experienced a blow-out en route as the spare tire mounted on the body of the coach by the driver is missing.—WHITE MOTOR CORPORATION

Rumbling westward through a tree-shaded Michigan City, Indiana, street, three big Pullman built interurbans operated a South Bend-Chicago limited schedule on a September afternoon in 1938.—WILLIAM C. JANSSEN (TOP RIGHT) On a bright winter day an eight-car South Bend train raced past Lake Park siding at Hudson Lake, Indiana. (CENTER RIGHT) In a classic tableau of winter railroading on the South Shore Line a South Bend limited is pictured in the snow-shrouded countryside of La Porte County, Indiana, near Hudson Lake in the late 1930's. The collective whine of 28 traction motors echoed from the side slopes of a long cut as a total of 9,600 h.p. urged the 11-car consist eastward. (LOWER RIGHT) Westbound for Chicago in November 1938, a two-car train of heavy steel coaches raced past the New Carlisle, Indiana, substation midway between South Bend and Michigan City.—ALL MWEH COLLECTION

The Insull companies were among the leaders in American industry in such fields as industrial safety, enlightened labor relations, and the development of effective public relations programs. The new South Shore management team brought with it skills in these areas that had already been intensely developed in the exceptionally successful Insull recovery program for the North Shore Line.

Safety was made the subject of intense interest by South Shore management. Safety awareness was encouraged among the railway's employees through such means as regular safety meetings; in 1928, for example, a total of 182 such meetings was attended by over 30,000 employees. Employee safety suggestions were actively solicited, and in 1928 alone 237 such suggestions were placed in effect. Many company employees were trained in first aid, and skilled South Shore first aid teams gave demonstrations for both company employees and the public. Several such teams participated in the Sixth Annual First Aid Championship Meet in Chicago in 1928.

Heroic acts by employees were recognized by such means as presentation of the Britton I. Budd Medal for the Saving of Human Life. Improvements in the railway's signal system and installation of fully protected crossings at many locations contributed to improved operating safety. Typical of the results of the South Shore safety program were those for 1928, when the company experienced a reduction of almost a third in lost-time hours from accidents over the preceeding year, despite an increase of over 100,000 hours in total working hours.

In keeping with the advanced labor principles practised by the Insull companies, the South Shore Line developed a broad program for better employee relations. More than half of the railway's employees took advantage of a group life and accident insurance plan developed by the South Shore, in which the company shared a portion of the cost. A free medical service for employees was established. Employee savings and investment funds were established. A Better Business Campaign provided prizes for business tips from employees; in 1927 over 4,000 tips leading to new business

The railway's booklet *First and Fastest*, gave details of the improved services that won the road the Coffin Medal and the *Electric Traction* speed trophy detailed on pages 68-69.— SOUTH BEND PUBLIC LIBRARY

were received. Employees were urged to promote the sale of company stock. Over 6,000 shares of South Shore stock were sold in 1928 through the efforts of employees in a customer ownership campaign, and more than 90 percent of the railway's employees bought company stock themselves. A new monthly employee magazine *The Pantagraph*, regularly included information on the South Shore's current advertising and publicity campaigns, encouraging employee support.

Employee social activities of every description were encouraged. The South Shore organized such events as all-employee parties, and offered a variety of educational and entertainment programs. Under an arrangement with Purdue University, for example, the railway paid half of tuition costs for employees enrolled in night school courses with the University's engineering extension department. A bowling

A remarkable contrast in electric railway equipment is provided by this view of Northern Indiana Railway birney car No. 602 passing a two-car train of South Shore's heavy steel interurbans on LaSalle Avenue at South Bend about 1937. (CENTER) A few of the original CLS&SB cars survived as work or service equipment on the new Chicago South Shore & South Bend. Re-equipped with D.C. motors and controls, Niles combine No. 73 remained in service until 1941 as work motor No. 1126. (BELOW) At South Bend the South Shore trains ran down the street in the traditional manner of the Midwest interurban. In this 1937 scene the train had just discharged passengers from the west and was heading down LaSalle Avenue to the storage yard. — ALL MWEH COLLECTION

A series of lithographed posters by leading Chicago artists was a distinguished feature of the South Shore's advertising program. "Homeward Bound by South Shore Line" by Oscar Rabe Hanson won two medals at a 1927 New York exhibition of advertising art.—ALL CHICAGO HISTORICAL SOCIETY

league, a basketball team, and the South Shore Line Men's Chorus were sponsored by the company. Employees trained in public speaking by the railway's Public Speakers Bureau aided the South Shore's promotional program.

The advertising, promotional, and public relations efforts of the new South Shore Line management seemed inexhaustible. A public relations staff issued a continuing series of South Shore news stories to newspapers, magazines, and other publications. A carefully planned advertising program was developed in close coordination with the South Shore's traffic department. Newspaper advertising featured popular events or resorts available by South Shore trains, service changes, special rates, parlor and dining services, or general institutional copy. Freight service was advertised on a national basis. Window displays in principal stations were used to promote special events or attractions along the South Shore. Billboards, electric signs, and posters were used in the railway's outdoor advertising program.

One of the most notable features of the South Shore advertising program was the railway's series of distinguished lithographed posters, which were published regularly for exhibition in company stations, on Chicago "L" platforms, and in schools and libraries in South Shore ter-

ritory. Designed by prominent Chicago artists, the poster series won wide distinction for its high artistic standards. One, "Homeward Bound by South Shore Line," by artist Oscar Rabe Hanson, won both the Art Directors Club and Baron Collier medals at the sixth annual exhibition of advertising art at the Art Center in New York City in 1927.

Promotional materials printed and distributed by the South Shore included folders, blotters, booklets, and other literature featuring the railway's services or points of interest. An eight-page monthly magazine, *South Shore Lines,* was distributed to the public in trains and stations, or by mail. In addition to traffic promotional material, the magazine included such information as listings of lost and found articles and athletic schedules.

A Public Speaking Bureau organized by the South Shore supplied trained speakers for talks of a public relations nature. A free motion picture library and lecture service was established by the South Shore, and several movies and a series of stereoptican films were produced, covering such varied topics as a history of Chicago area transportation, the Field Museum, the Union Stockyards, vacation areas along the South Shore, and the railway's block signal system.

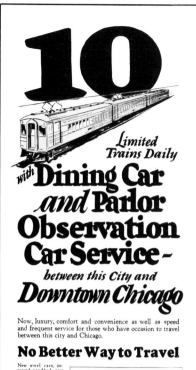

10
Limited Trains Daily
with **Dining Car and Parlor Observation Car Service —**
between this City and
Downtown Chicago

Now, luxury, comfort and convenience as well as speed and frequent service for those who have occasion to travel between this city and Chicago.

No Better Way to Travel

New steel cars, improved roadbed, new automatic block signals, more trains, faster running time, no smoke, no cinders.

Good meals in the dining cars. Service a la carte. Light refreshments served in the parlor-observation cars.

Ride in a parlor-observation car or eat a meal in a dining car the next time you travel on the South Shore Line. You will enjoy it. The parlor cars are divided into cozy homelike compartments—private smoking rooms for men and private rest room for women. Glass enclosed observation platform.

All South Shore Line trains are electrically operated from South Bend to downtown Chicago—(Terminal station: Randolph Street at Michigan Avenue.)

A train to Chicago every hour on the hour from 5 a.m. to 9 p.m., then 11 p.m.

Schedule of Dining Car and Parlor-Observation Car Trains

	Fort Dearborn Limited	Grant Park Limited	Illinois Limited	Randolph Limited	Garden City Limited
	AM	AM	Noon	PM	PM
Lv. South Bend	7:00	10:00	12:00	3:00	5:00
Lv. New Carlisle	7:23	10:23	12:23	3:23	5:23
Lv. Michigan City	7:51	10:51	12:51	3:51	5:51
Lv. Tremont (Gateway to Indiana Dunes State Park)	8:06	11:06	1:06	4:06	6:06
Lv. Gary	8:30	11:30	1:30	4:30	6:30
Lv. East Chicago	8:45	11:45	1:45	4:45	6:45
Lv. Hammond	8:51	11:51	1:51	4:51	6:51
Ar. (Randolph St.) Downtown Chicago	9:30	12:30	2:30	5:30	7:30
	AM	PM	PM	PM	PM

	Notre Dame Limited	Dune-land Limited	Indiana Limited	Marquette Limited	St. Joe Valley Limited
	AM	AM	Noon	PM	PM
Lv. Downtown Chicago (Randolph St.)	7:00	10:00	12:00	3:00	
Lv. Hammond	7:35	10:35	12:35	3:35	5:35
Lv. East Chicago	7:41	10:41	12:41	3:41	5:41
Lv. Gary	8:00	11:00	1:00	4:00	6:00
Lv. Tremont (Gateway to Indiana Dunes State Park)	8:21	11:21	1:21	4:21	6:21
Lv. Michigan City	8:37	11:37	1:37	4:37	6:37
Lv. New Carlisle	9:07	12:07	2:07	5:07	7:07
Ar. South Bend	9:33	12:33	2:33	5:33	7:33
	AM	PM	PM	PM	PM

A.M. figures in light face type; P.M. figures in bold face type.
*—Stops on signal to receive and discharge passengers.
In Chicago, all trains stop at Van Buren, Roosevelt Road (Central Station, Fifty-third St., Sixty-third St. and Kensington. South Shore Line-Illinois Central Suburban stations. "Dining Car X Parlor Car. "Transfer at Michigan City to South Shore Line Motor Coaches for Western Michigan Points.

Chicago South Shore & South Bend Railroad
A. J. Bankson, Ticket Agent
301 North Michigan, Phone Main

Two trains an hour, now 69 Daily —
to and from downtown
CHICAGO

TAKE your choice of 69 trains that run each day to and from downtown Chicago.

Service every half hour during the day for busy men and women. Travel without loss of time or waiting. See the schedule at the left for time of departure for and arrival in Chicago (Randolph Street).

The new service added to handle the increased traffic.

From Gary, Hammond and East Chicago they operate on a half hourly basis, maintaining fast scheduling as the Chicago Expresses.

Through hourly trains from South Bend to the Chicago Loop will continue to be called Chicago Limiteds to distinguish them from the Expresses.

During the night hours service will continue as in the past.

South Shore Line trains run between this city and the Illinois Central-South Shore Line Suburban Station at Randolph and Michigan Avenue, within easy walking distance of hotels, theatres and department stores.

Stops are made at Kensington, 63rd Street (Woodlawn), 53rd Street (Hyde Park), Roosevelt Road (12th Street) and Van Buren.

Chicago South Shore & South Bend Railroad

SOUTH SHORE LINE

Clean, cinderless, smokeless—electrified all the way.
New Steel Passenger Cars.
Use money-saving commutation fares—a ticket for every type of user.

Chicago invites you
for a happy vacation
Memorial Day — Monday, May 30 *week-end!*

THREE wonderful days are yours over Memorial week-end. Enjoy them in Chicago, where every amusement awaits you!

Take the fast, clean, and comfortable South Shore Line direct to Chicago. A train leaves the South Bend terminal (301 N. Michigan St.) every hour on the hour. This splendid service brings you right into the heart of the Loop.

The South Shore Line is the carefree way to travel; avoid congested highways!

Things to See and Do

[list of attractions]

40 Limited Trains daily
now in Service—20 each way to and from Chicago. Twelve luxurious new parlor-observation and dining cars supply every travel comfort. Parlor car seats only 15c extra between any two points. Dining car trains leave South Bend at 6 A.M., 11 A.M., and 5 P.M. Parlor observation with buffet service, leave at 7 A.M., 12 Noon, and 4 P.M. For further information phone Main 0440.

Chicago South Shore & South Bend Railroad

SOUTH SHORE LINE

All trains operate on Central Standard Time.

SOUTH SHORE LINE

to the theatre
to the shops

Trains for Business for Shoppers for Pleasure
Every Half Hour
to and from Chicago

Men and women en route to or from Downtown Chicago now get double the service on the South Shore Line.

South Shore Line trains, running every thirty minutes from morning to evening, give this city unrivaled transportation to and from Chicago.

Sixty-Nine Trains a Day

The new trains added to carry the rapidly increasing traffic, have been named Chicago Expresses. Through trains from South Bend and Michigan City are still called Limiteds. The Chicago Expresses operate between Gary, Hammond and East Chicago and the Loop.

Fast schedules, affording unusually convenient service will be maintained by both expresses and limiteds. Night service continues as before.

South Shore Line trains make six stops at advantageous points in Chicago, Kensington, 63rd Street (Woodlawn), 53rd Street (Hyde Park), Roosevelt Road (12th Street), Van Buren and Randolph Suburban Station of the Illinois Central-South Shore Line at Michigan Avenue.

Chicago South Shore & South Bend Railroad

SOUTH SHORE LINE

Clean, cinderless, smokeless—electrified all the way.
New Steel Passenger Cars.
Use money-saving commutation fares—a ticket for every type of user.

Reproduced here are examples of the newspaper advertisements used by the South Shore in its vigorous promotional program to acquaint the riding public with their trains and deluxe service.—ALL WAYNE C. OLSEN COLLECTION

A miniature South Shore Line working model was built by the railway's electrical department for public exhibit. Operating over a 69-foot track, the highly detailed display included models of the South Shore's freight and passenger equipment, which drew power from an overhead catenary system. At the Greater Gary and East Chicago-Indiana Harbor expositions in 1927, the exhibit drew some 50,000 visitors.

With the North Shore Line and the Chicago, Aurora & Elgin Railroad, which came under Insull control in 1926, the South Shore opened an Outing and Recreation Bureau and an Own Your Own Home Bureau in Chicago, which provided information concerning points of interest, resorts, vacation spots, and home sites along the three interurbans, and were staffed to assist travelers in making all necessary arrangements. In 1927 some 550 agents of the Chicago Rapid Transit Company and the Illinois Central's suburban service were taken on a day's outing over South Shore's rail and motor coach lines. By gaining first-hand knowledge of South Shore services, reasoned the railway, these men would help sell its services to potential Chicago-area travelers.

Particular effort went into the promotion of traffic to and from the resorts and recreation spots reached by the South Shore. Special party business in particular was vigorously and successfully promoted. In 1928, for example, the railway scheduled some 250 special movements which handled nearly 15,000 persons on picnic outings, lodge specials, church and school parties, and similar excursions. By means of a special arrangement with the Chicago Y.M.C.A. some 1,750 "Y" members were transported to and from a summer camp at Forest Beach on Lake Michigan, moving via South Shore trains between Chicago and Michigan City, with motor coaches of the subsidiary Shore Line Motor Coach Company providing the connection to Forest Beach. To help promote the special travel arrangement the South Shore published a special Forest Beach folder.

Typical of the means employed to promote special movement travel was the publication,

No recreational attraction along the South Shore was more popular than the celebrated Indiana Dunes area at the south end of Lake Michigan, and none was more extensively promoted by the railway. Posters, a Duneland folder, maps of hiking trails, and frequent newspaper advertising were all employed to promote interest in the Dunes, and the South Shore played an important role in the establishment of the Indiana Dunes State Park.— INDIANA STATE LIBRARY AND STEPHEN D. MAGUIRE COLLECTION

Picnic Places Along the South Shore Line, aimed principally at company picnic committee chairmen, which detailed the attractions of such on-line picnic areas as Hudson Lake, Washington Park, and Grand Beach.

By far the most popular South Shore recreation spot, however, was the famous Indiana Dunes area along Lake Michigan between Gary and Michigan City, and the railway's greatest promotional efforts were directed to the development of traffic to the Dunes. The South Shore worked closely with the Indiana State Park Commission in efforts to protect the Dunes area from industrialization and to establish the 2,000-acre Indiana Dunes State Park. Plans were made to construct a spur track into the park, and the railway contributed $25,000 to a fund for the construction of a resort hotel and bath house in the Park at Waverly.

The attractions of the Dunes Park were regularly featured in South Shore posters, advertising, and promotional literature, such as a special map-folder which showed hiking trails in the Park. Advertising featured the slogan "See the Dunes Afoot" to encourage train riding rather than automobile travel to the Dunes. Special weekend and three-day excursion fares to the Dunes Park were offered.

Construction of what was claimed to be the country's largest structural steel ski slide immediately adjacent to the railway at Ogden Dunes, eight miles east of Gary, gave the South Shore still another recreational attraction. In addition to supporting its construction, the South Shore featured the ski slide extensively in its advertising program, and even built a miniature of the slide which was exhibited at various locations in Chicago.

To supplement the commuter and short haul traffic that constituted the majority of its passenger business, the South Shore Line made a number of innovations intended to encourage the long distance traveler. Through ticketing arrangements were made with the North Shore Line, and for passengers originating on South Shore the railway would obtain railroad and Pullman tickets and even deliver them to the prospective passenger. Arrangements were made with transfer companies to check baggage through to its ultimate destination, or directly to their homes for terminating passengers. A few years later South Shore agents began selling through rail-air tickets via South Shore and the Chicago-based services of United Air Lines, American Airways, and Trans-American Air Lines.

After the CI&L Railway (Monon Route) discontinued passenger service over its branch into Michigan City in 1928, the South Shore and the Monon developed a through ticketing arrangement between all points on the South Shore and Monon points in central and southern Indiana. Passengers transferred between trains of the two companies at Hammond, Indiana, where a free taxicab transfer was provided for passengers and baggage.

Even after the initial rehabilitation of the property had been concluded, the South Shore's new Insull management continued to invest substantial capital in a further program of physical improvements which would permit the railway to handle its steadily growing vol-

Another in the series of lithographed posters was this interesting Ski Meet notice.—CHICAGO HISTORICAL SOCIETY

63

ume of passenger and freight traffic with increased speed and efficiency.

Upgrading of the railway's track structure continued without interruption. By the fall of 1927, barely two years after the new management had assumed control, 70 pound rail had been replaced with 100 pound sections on 30 miles of track. Almost half that mileage had been rock ballasted, and another 2,000 carloads of cinder ballast installed. More than 67,000 creosoted red oak ties had been laid to replace old ties.

In addition to the initial program for double-ending sidings and equipping them with high-speed turnouts to permit high speed meets, key sidings were lengthened to permit greater flexibility in meeting times. The siding at Wilson, Indiana, a principal single track meeting point between Gary and Michigan City, was lengthened to two and one-half miles, permitting a flexibility of six minutes in the meeting time of trains. Another 4,200 foot siding at Tamarack, five miles west of Michigan City, was equipped with No. 20 turnouts and spring switches, which permitted passage of trains at speeds as high as 60 m.p.h. A number of other regular meeting points were also equipped with spring switches, which permitted a meet to be made without stopping to set switches. In order to relieve congestion at Gary, the eastern end of the South Shore's double track installation, an additional 3,300 feet of double track was laid east of the Gary station.

The railway's entire semaphore block signal system, which had been rehabilitated under the initial reconstruction program as an interim measure, was replaced less than two years later with a new Union Switch & Signal Company color light block signal system. A number of special signal installations were made to permit greater speed in the handling of traffic at critical locations. Special signals at gauntlet track installations over bridges on the double track line gave what amounted to automatic interlocking protection, allowing operation of the gauntlets as virtually double track line. Another special installation made in 1928 provided for dispatcher control of the passing track signals at Davis, just east of Michigan City. To assist a late eastbound train to regain schedule, the dispatcher could hold a westbound train at Davis for the eastbound, since a

Built at a cost of over $200,000, this handsome joint rail-bus terminal was opened at Michigan City in May 1927. Passengers transferred here between South Shore trains and buses of the subsidiary Shore Line Motor Coach Company operating to points in southwestern Michigan.—BALDWIN LOCOMOTIVES MAGAZINE

westbound run had a greater opportunity to regain time. Still another special installation at the west end of Gary siding permitted trains to line up a clear route over a main line gauntlet bridge to the west, assuring heavy freights an opportunity to make a run for the grade leading to the bridge.

Late in May 1927 the South Shore opened a handsome new joint rail-bus station at Michigan City, which represented not only a major traffic point on the railway but the principal transfer point between South Shore trains and buses of the subsidiary Shore Line Motor Coach Company as well. Constructed at a cost of over $200,000, the new station included a spacious waiting room with large ticket and information booths for train and bus passengers, a men's smoking room, a "large and artistically furnished" ladies' lounge, a luncheonette counter, and separate parcel and baggage rooms. Doors in the front of the building led to the street where trains stopped to load passengers, while doors in the rear led to the platforms used by buses of the Shore Line company, as well as several independent motor coach lines. The facade of the station was finished in a handsome buff colored terra cotta, while the interior finish included handsome marble faced columns, and oak trim and waiting benches finished in weathered green.

The second floor of the building contained office spaces for the motor coach company as well as a large meeting hall capable of accommodating 200 persons for employee activities. The basement contained shower and locker facilities for trainmen and bus company employees. Adjoining the new station to the east was a new main garage for the Shore Line company. Large enough to accommodate 30 buses, the garage incorporated the latest features and equipment for efficient motor coach maintenance.

Formal opening of the station and garage on Saturday evening, May 21st, was the occasion for gala celebration. To entertain the crowd of over 12,000 people that visited the new facility an orchestra played for dancing in the station proper, while the Chicago Rapid Transit Band gave a concert in the garage. Company officials were on hand to explain the new facilities, and favors were given to all lady visitors.

Although the former South Bend station had been remodeled less than two years before, the South Shore opened a rebuilt and enlarged station at South Bend early in 1928. In order to accommodate the railway's greatly increased passenger traffic, the new facility was more than three times the size of the former station. Architectural features of the new terminal were patterned after those of the new Michigan City station. Facilities for beverage and light lunch services, operated by the South Shore, were installed in the new South Bend station as well as several other principal stations.

The South Shore's massive reconstruction program, which by the end of 1927 represented an investment of close to $6.5 million, had enabled the railway to carry out some phenomenal improvements in its services. Passenger service had been increased from a schedule of some 35 daily trains in 1925 to a total of 81 trains by the spring of 1928. An hourly service was offered between Chicago and South Bend from the early morning hours until almost midnight, while half hourly service was operated between Chicago and Gary during the same period. The journey between Chicago and South Bend, which had required a minimum of 2 hours 55 minutes in 1925, was being operated on limited schedules requiring as little as 2 hours 10 minutes by the spring of 1927. Development of additional interchange points with steam railroads, construction of new or enlarged freight stations, and the purchase of new freight locomotives and equipment had permitted an equally significant improvement in the quality of South Shore freight service.

The benefits of the Insull reconstruction program were reflected in glowing statistics in one annual report after another. Passenger traffic increased from a level of little more than a million and a half passengers in 1925 to nearly three million riders annually by 1928, while passenger revenues increased by almost 200 percent during the same three-year period. Freight revenues, which had totaled less than

$200,000 in 1925, exceeded a million dollars for the first time in 1928, a three-year increase of some 535 percent. Gross operating revenues, which had totaled slightly under $860,000 in 1925, reached an annual level of well over two million dollars by 1927, and increased again to more than three million dollars in 1928.

It was a time of unparalleled success for the one-time hard luck interurban, and there seemed ample cause for such confident statements as that by South Shore president Britton I. Budd in 1927, "Well located interurban lines, instead of being obsolete, are in reality entering upon the period of their greatest usefulness."

To keep pace with its steadily growing volume of passenger traffic, the South Shore ordered still more new equipment in 1928. Ten steel passenger motor coaches, identical with the Pullman units delivered the year before, were ordered from the Standard Steel Car Company of Hammond, Indiana, in May. A second ten-car order placed with Standard six months later included five motor passenger coaches, three coach trailers, and two parlor trailers.

Although the hard work of rebuilding the railroad and developing its traffic to a profitable level characterized the South Shore Line of the late 1920's, there were some lighter moments as well. The South Shore's retired passenger traffic manager, R. E. Jamieson, who joined the railroad in 1926, recently recalled some of them.

Excursion traffic, of course, had always been important to the South Shore. Because extra trains and large crowds were usually involved, things always seemed a little more likely to go wrong whenever special movements were scheduled.

One of the first large special excursions handled by the new South Shore management was the movement of 3,100 students, faculty, and guests from South Bend to Chicago for a Notre Dame-Northwestern football game at Evanston in 1926. The railroad's new equipment had not yet been delivered, and much of its rehabilitation work had yet to be completed. Consequently, the unusually large movement

taxed the railroad's facilities to the limit.

The westbound moves were made without mishap, and all went well on the return trip until a special carrying some 500 students arrived at Bendix, just out of South Bend, where it was scheduled to meet a westbound dead-heading equipment run. The westbound train had run into difficulties without ever leaving South Bend, and the student special waited interminably at Bendix. While the dispatcher refused to break the meet the time reached 11 p.m. and then midnight, the Notre Dame deadline for students. Conductor Bob Reppert even offered to walk in front of the train flagging with a red lantern, but the dispatcher was relentless and refused to let the train move. It took most of the night before the mess was straightened out and the special finally crept into South Bend.

The next morning Jamieson appeared before Father Hugh O'Donnell at Notre Dame and took the blame for the railroad to clear the 500 students of rule infractions at the University. During an investigation of the affair at headquarters in Michigan City superintendent Gray asked conductor Reppert, "Did you call the dispatcher?" "Yes, Mr. Gray," chimed in trainmaster Merle Anton, who had listened in on the conductor's calls the night before, "he called him everything."

Typical of the mishaps that could snarl up a special movement was one that occured during a heavy movement for a Notre Dame-Minnesota football game at South Bend during the 1920's. Five special trains carrying fans to the game became too closely bunched not far from South Bend and blew the circuit breakers in the Grandview Substation. Before the power supply could be restored five trainloads of irate football fans had missed the first quarter.

Things could go wrong on the company's bus subsidiary, too. Passenger man Jamieson recalls one July 4th, when the South Shore promoted as excursion to Detriot, using buses beyond Michigan City. About 2 p.m. one driver called in from Fort Wayne to ask "How in the hell do I get to Detroit from here?"

One special run that was carried out without any unscheduled mishaps, at least, was what

An infrequent sight on South Shore was the operation of Pullman sleeping car equipment. This standard sleeper attached to a *Notre Dame Limited* at South Bend was probably operated for the benefit of an athletic team.—O. F. LEE COLLECTION

Still more equipment was delivered to the South Shore in 1929 by the Standard Steel Car Company, which completed an order for 18 coaches and 2 parlor cars. Car No. 40 was delivered as a coach trailer, but had been converted to a motor car by time this photograph was taken in 1946. (BELOW) Headed by coach trailer No. 201, a two-car Chicago express thunders across the Calumet River bridge near Ford City in the summer of 1938.—BOTH MWEH COLLECTION

was perhaps the most unusual special train ever handled by the South Shore. Mr. Bendix of the Bendix Corporation at South Bend wanted something different for a sales meeting he was planning, and the South Shore obligingly put together a train of four battered open platform coaches hauled by a borrowed steam engine. A train crew dressed in "Gay '90's" regalia ran the train from the sales meeting in the LaSalle Hotel, through the streets of South Bend, and out to Chain Lakes and return. A news butcher peddled shriveled oranges and old papers and magazines aboard the train. Except for the delay caused by a fake farmer who had tethered his cow along the track, the trip was made without incident except for the fun that Bendix and his salesmen had.

Jamieson still remembers vividly one night in 1931 when he was in charge of a special train transporting the great traction tycoon Samuel Insull himself. Insull had traveled to South Bend to address the Chicago Club of Notre Dame in a meeting held on the University campus.

The special train, made up of two motor cars and a parlor car, left South Bend on the return trip to Chicago at about 11 p.m. With a clear track, the extra raced toward Chicago at high speed, but Insull was tired and impatient. As the train approached Smith's Hill a few miles east of Hudson Lake at close to 90 m.p.h. a porter summoned Jamieson to the parlor car where Insull was riding.

"Jamieson," said Insull, "can't you make this damn train go any faster?' One never said "No" to Mr. Insull, so Jamieson said, "I'll see what I can do, Sir," and went up to the cab. Jack Teets was the motorman and when Jamieson gave him the "old man's" request, Teets indicated that he had the controller up against the brass and that the train was doing better than 85 m.p.h.

Teets, however, was equal to the occasion. He started kicking on about ten pounds of air, then kicking it right off again. As a result, the train developed a pronounced vibration and the speed was reduced about 15 m.p.h. The vibration produced the desired effect, for when

Jamieson presented himself to the tycoon, Insull commented, "That's fine, Jamieson."

The advent of the South Shore's heavy, powerful steel passenger cars, as well as the railway's continuing program of improvements to track, passing sidings, and its signalling system, had enabled South Shore to progressively increase its operating speeds from 1926 onward.

Prior to the inauguration of through service into the Chicago Loop over the Illinois Central Suburban electrification in 1926, even the fastest available schedules had required 2 hours 55 minutes for the journey between Chicago and South Bend, with most express schedules requiring three hours or more. Through operation to the Loop with South Shore's new steel equipment permitted substantial improvements in Chicago-South Bend timings. By early 1927 typical limited train schedules called for a 2 hour 30 minute timing, with the railway's fastest train, a late evening South Bend Limited, carded over the line in only 2 hours 10 minutes. Within another year, although the majority of limited schedules remained at 2 hours 30 minutes, a number of the South Shore's extra fast limiteds were being operated on 2 hours 15 minutes timings. Still another tightening of schedules in the fall of 1928 reduced the standard limited train timing to 2 hours 20 minutes between Chicago and South Bend, with extra fast trains operating on 2 hour 5 minute timings.

Ever since the private automobile had begun to represent a growing threat to interurban railway passenger traffic in the years following World War I, an increasing number of leaders in the traction industry had come to regard high speed service as one of the most important measures by which they could maintain a competitive edge over highway travel. Foremost among the advocates of high speed operation during the early 1920's were the editors of *Electric Traction* magazine, one of the two leading industry trade journals. Speed, editorialized *Electric Traction,* was the primary factor in the public's choice of travel mode. Comfort, luxury, and even safety were of secondary consideration.

Even as early as 1924, a year before the railway's reorganization and reconstruction under Insull management, the South Shore's fastest Kensington-South Bend timings gave the railway a respectable seventh place ranking in a national interurban speed tabulation compiled by *Electric Traction.* By 1927, after the inauguration of through service into Chicago with its new equipment, the South Shore's 2 hour 10 minute fastest timing between Chicago and South Bend had gained the railway a national speed ranking second only to the North Shore in what had become an annual interurban speed contest sponsored jointly by *Electric Traction* and the American Electric Railway Association.

The South Shore's speed contest ranking remained unchanged the following year, but in 1929 a further acceleration of its fastest Chicago-South Bend timing to two hours flat enabled the railway to take possession of the handsome silver *Electric Traction* interurban speed trophy from the North Shore Line, which had held it for the two previous years. The South Shore's contest-winning 45 m.p.h. terminal-to-terminal average speed represented an increase of no less than 33 percent in the average speed of the railway's fastest schedules within a period of only three years.

An even more prestigious award for the South Shore in 1929 was the railway's selection as the seventh annual recipient of the Charles A. Coffin prize. The Coffin award was provided by the Charles A. Coffin Foundation, which had been established in 1922 by the board of directors of the General Electric Company in honor of the company's first and long-time president. The annual prize, which included presentation of the Charles A. Coffin Gold Medal to the company and a gift of $1,000 to its employees' benefit or a similar fund, was awarded by a committee of the American Electric Railway Association "to that electric railway company in the United States which during the year has made the greatest contribution toward increasing the advantage of electric transportation for the convenience and well-being of the public and for the benefit of the industry."

In 1929 South Shore won both the Charles A. Coffin Medal "for distinguished contribution to the development of electric transportation for the convenience of the public and the benefit of the industry", and the *Electric Traction* interurban speed trophy for the fastest regular schedules between terminals.—ED WOJTAS COURTESY OF TRAINS MAGAZINE AND WILLIAM D. MIDDLETON COLLECTION

Selection of the South Shore for the award was made by the AERA's 1929 Coffin Prize committee after reviewing the phenomenal improvements in service and operating results brought about by the Insull reconstruction program. "Within four years the Chicago South Shore and South Bend Railroad, —" noted the committee, "has moved figuratively from the scrap heap to the front rank among the electric railways of America."

Both the speed trophy and the Coffin Prize were presented to the South Shore at the October 1929 annual convention of the American Electric Railway Association in Atlantic City. The South Shore's efficient publicity organization made the most of the dual presentation. Impressive six-column advertisements in Chicago and northern Indiana newspapers featured the two awards and depicted the services that had won them. Articles about the awards were featured in *South Shore Lines* and *The Pantagraph*, the railway's monthly magazines distributed to the public and employees. A handsome booklet, *First and Fastest*, was printed for wide public distribution. In the Chicago area South Shore joined with the two other major Insull interurbans, the North Shore Line and the Chicago, Aurora & Elgin Railroad, in an extensive billboard, poster, and card advertising campaign on the Chicago "L" and surface car systems, as well as newspaper advertising, featuring the fact that the three roads had captured the first three places in the 1929 *Electric Traction* national interurban speed contest.

The South Shore's publicity organization made the most of the railroad's two prestigious 1929 awards. Reproduced is a six-column ad used to publicize the awards in major Chicago area newspapers. — ELECTRIC TRACTION MAGAZINE

Receipt of the two distinguished industry awards highlighted what was to prove one of the greatest years in the entire history of the South Shore Line. Traffic and revenues for 1929 increased again over even the remarkable level of 1928. Passenger traffic reached a new peak of almost three and a quarter million passengers, and passenger revenues passed the two million dollar level for the first time. Freight revenues of nearly $1.6 million represented an increase of close to 30 percent over the previous year. Gross operating revenues for the year were almost $3.7 million, an increase of some 330 percent over the 1925 level.

If 1929 seemed the best of all possible years for the South Shore, disturbing doubts for the future were raised by the catastrophic events in the New York stock market late in the year.

The effects of the great Wall Street crash of 1929 and the great national depression that followed it were by no means immediately felt by the South Shore Line. Although the exhilarating increases of the previous five years failed to continue, operating results for 1930 were only slightly off the record level of 1929. Passenger traffic dropped off to a level of three million passengers, but the decline in revenues was at least partially offset by a modest increase in freight revenues over those for the previous year. Gross operating revenues for the year remained above $3.5 million, and net income was down by only a little over $100,000.

Still optimistic for the future, the South Shore continued to undertake major improvements to the property during 1930. A large new shop building of some 32,000 square feet, including the latest available equipment for heavy rolling stock repair and overhaul, was placed under construction at Michigan City. The original shop building, which had served the South Shore since its opening in 1908, was rebuilt for use as an inspection and painting facility. Confident of continuing traffic growth, South Shore built a facility that could adequately care for a much larger fleet of cars and locomotives.

A new freight terminal was placed under construction at South Bend. Three 85-ton freight locomotives were ordered from the General Electric Company, and another 80-ton Baldwin-Westinghouse unit was ordered for delivery in 1931.

By 1931, however, there was no longer any doubt about the effect of Depression conditions on the South Shore. Passenger traffic fell abruptly to a level of some 2.2 million passengers, the lowest since 1926. Freight revenues dropped below the $1.5 million level for the

first time since 1928. Gross operating revenues for the year were down to $2.9 million. Even at that, the South Shore managed to post a modest net income of $115,000.

If 1931 was bad, 1932 was a disaster. Passenger traffic plummeted downward again to less than 1.5 million, the lowest level since the earliest years of the predecessor Chicago, Lake Shore & South Bend Ry. Freight revenues declined almost as severely, to less than a million dollars. Gross operating revenues for the year were less than $1.9 million, and the South Shore posted a 1932 net loss of almost half a million dollars.

Despite its rapidly declining fortunes, the South Shore continued to maintain a high standard of service. In 1930 the railway cut its fastest Chicago-South Bend timing to a new low of 1 hour 58 minutes, and retained the *Electric Traction* speed trophy for a second year. Even though the North Shore Line regained

This six-column advertisement prepared for the South Shore Line after winning of the Coffin award and Speed Trophy appeared in Michigan City and South Bend, Indiana, newspapers showing various instances of South Shore Line's distinguished service to the area.
—ELECTRIC TRACTION MAGAZINE

possession of the trophy in 1933 with even greater accelerations, the South Shore continued to improve its high speed performance during the early Depression years. In 1931 another five minutes was cut from the fastest schedules, to give the South Shore an average schedule speed of almost 48 m.p.h. over the 90-mile Chicago-South Bend run. By 1933 the best timing had been cut to only 1 hour 50 minutes, a terminal-to-terminal average of over 49 m.p.h.

Even into early 1932 the South Shore continued to schedule no less than 80 daily trains, 11 of which offered dining or parlor car service. The only apparent concessions to depression conditions were the $1 luncheons and $1.50 dinners offered on dining car menus.

But by the spring of 1932 Depression realities could no longer be avoided. Drastic cuts in passenger service were ordered, and dining and parlor car service vanished from South Shore timetables for good. The once expansive operations of the South Shore's motor coach subsidiary, which had been merged into the railway in 1930, suffered even more drastically. By 1932 motor coach services had been reduced to only four daily round trips over a single route between Michigan City and Benton Harbor, Michigan.

Operating results for 1933 were even worse than the preceeding year. While passenger traffic remained almost at the 1932 level, freight revenues declined to a new low of barely $800,000. Although gross operating revenues were down to less than $1.7 million, reductions in operating costs held the net loss for the year to less than $360,000.

The great Insull public utilities empire survived the first few years of the Depression with-

Pullman-built coach No. 8 waited for a run at Gary in the spring of 1946. Part of the Insull management's initial new car order delivered in 1926. No. 8 and most of her running mates never received the South Shore's post-World War II lengthening and modernization program.—WILLIAM C. JANSSEN

This was electric railroading in the grand manner. Five pantographs reached for the compound catenary as an eastbound seven-car train of heavy steel multiple-unit coaches bore down on Lydick, Indiana, on an autumn day in 1938.—MWEH COLLECTION

out difficulty. But a financial crisis in 1932 forced one of the keystones of the Insull empire, Middle West Utilities, into bankruptcy. Soon afterward, Sam Insull was forced out of the management of his remaining interests, and the great Insull utilities empire collapsed. The South Shore, with the heavy losses of 1932 and 1933, proved no less vulnerable than the remainder of the Insull empire.

Dividends had never been paid on South Shore common stock, and early in 1932 dividends were suspended even on the railway's preferred stock. On September 30, 1933, the South Shore entered bankruptcy.

Once again the South Shore Line had hit bottom in the roller coaster course of its corporate fortunes. The exhilarating years of the Insull era were past, and the business at hand was now that of survival itself.

73

3

THE
SOUTH SHORE
TRANSFORMED

IF THE immediate financial prospects that faced the newly bankrupt South Shore in 1933 were anything but encouraging, the Insull reconstruction and re-equipment program had at least left the railroad with a superb physical plant that could safely weather a few lean years. And however depressed its traffic levels, the South Shore was still taking in gross revenues well in excess of anything ever recorded in the pre-Insull years.

In any case, the dismal traffic figures of 1933 proved to be the worst the Depression had to offer, and thereafter the South Shore's fortunes began to show steady improvement. By 1937 gross revenues were back up to a level of some $2.5 million annually from the 1933 low of less than $1.7 million, and the railroad was again showing a modest net income. By early 1938 a satisfactory plan of reorganization had been worked out and the South Shore's bankruptcy was ended.

Heading the reorganized South Shore was Jay Samuel Hartt, a Chicago consulting engineer and Midland Utilities executive. During the record 21 years he was to head the South Shore, Sam Hartt would hold the railroad firmly on a course of continued reconstruction and improvement that would complete the Insull-begun transformation of the one-time electric interurban into a railroad scarcely distinguishable from a heavy trunk line electrification.

Coach No. 12 leads an eastbound commuter into the Hammond, Indiana, station. — JOHN GRUBER (OPPOSITE PAGE) Led by coach No 1, Chicago-Michigan City train No. 215 races over the Elgin, Joliet & Eastern overcrossing east of East Chicago, Indiana. Trailing the two coaches was a South Shore baggage car rebuilt from a former Indiana Railroad railway post office car.—WILLIAM D. MIDDLETON.

Elected president of South Shore in August 1939, electrical engineer and utilities executive Jay Samuel Hartt headed the railroad as president until 1960 and continued as chairman of the board until shortly before his death in 1962.—FABIAN BACHRACH FROM CSS&SB (BELOW) Headed by a pair of 80-ton Baldwin-Westinghouse motors of 1920's origin, an eastbound South Shore freight rumbled through the residential streets at Michigan City, Indiana, in June of 1947.—WILLIAM C. JANSSEN (OPPOSITE PAGE) Late in the autumn of 1938 a three-car train sped westward across the La Porte County countryside on South Shore single track, at Hicks, a few miles west of Hudson Lake.—MWEH COLLECTION

If there were few significant physical changes in the South Shore during the troubled 1930's, there were nonetheless several important developments in the South Shore's integration into the steam railroad community. Much of the new freight traffic developed under Insull management had consisted of "captive" tonnage controlled by other Insull companies; in the early 1930's close to three quarters of South Shore freight traffic was made up of coal, most of it destined for consumption in the plants of Insull utilities firms. Recognizing the need for a much broader base of general interline freight traffic, the new South Shore management set out to strengthen its freight solicitation efforts both in its own territory and through the establishment of a number of off-line freight agencies, a move that was to prove vital to the railroad's future. In the passenger department, too, South Shore moved toward closer alignment with steam railroads, when it began participating in interline passenger ticketing with steam lines for the first time in 1937.

Perhaps indicative of the South Shore's progressing transformation was a 1936 decision in a labor case by the Interstate Commerce Commission, which ruled that the company was not a street, interurban, or suburban electrical railway within the exemption provisions of the Railway Labor Act.

By the beginning of the 1940's South Shore traffic was again up to the levels of the Insull era. By 1940 freight revenues were the highest since 1931, and by 1941 annual freight revenues of over $1.8 million surpassed even the previous record year of 1930. Passenger traffic was picking up, too. By 1941 passenger volume had climbed to more than two and a quarter million, the South Shore's best passenger year since 1930.

But all of this was nothing compared to what the outbreak of war on December 7, 1941, would bring. As the heavily industrialized northwestern Indiana region geared up for maximum wartime production, South Shore traffic set one record after another. By 1943 passenger traffic had doubled the 1941 level. By 1945 South Shore's annual passenger volume had passed the six million mark — almost double that of 1929, the record year of the Insull era. Annual freight revenues had exceeded two million dollars by 1942, and stayed well above that level for the remainder of the war years.

In 1942 the South Shore began an extensive lengthening and modernization program for its steel passenger cars. First out of the shops was coach No. 15, which was lengthened by 17 feet 6 inches and increased in seating capacity from 56 to 80 passengers. The exterior colors were an experimental reversal of the normal South Shore orange and maroon. Interiors of the rebuilt cars were furnished with foam rubber seats, fluorescent lighting, and modernized baggage racks and ceilings. —BOTH MWEH COLLECTION (BELOW) Car No. 100, the first South Shore combination baggage-passenger car to be lengthened and modernized — in 1943 — emerged from the shops with a special red, white and blue "Buy War Bonds" color scheme.—DONALD DUKE COLLECTION

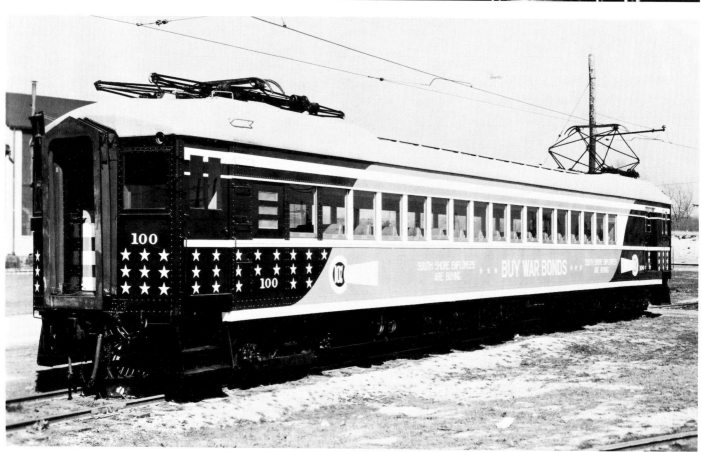

South Shore beefed up its freight motive power roster in 1941 with the purchase of four used 97-ton Baldwin-Westinghouse locomotives from the Illinois Central. The extra power came just in time for the unprecedented freight tonnage of World War II. Two of the 900-class head a short westbound freight at Portage, a few miles west of South Bend.—MWEH COLLECTION

For the South Shore it was an embarassment of riches. Additional equipment was virtually unobtainable, and somehow the railroad had to accommodate its unprecedented freight and passenger volume with largely the same fleet of cars and locomotives and the same physical plant that it had operated since the late 1920's.

For freight operations some measure of relief had been obtained in 1941 with the purchase of four used electric locomotives from the Illinois Central. The even greater surge in passenger traffic presented South Shore with the much more difficult problem of transporting more than twice the normal volume without any increase in its passenger car fleet. The railroad's rather ingenious solution was to simply enlarge its existing equipment. Except for their short 60 or 61 foot length, the heavy steel passenger cars of the Insull era were constructed to dimensions and standards generally comparable to steam railroad equipment, and motors and trucks were ample to take care of the increased weight represented by extending the car body length by 17 feet 6 inches.

The rebuilding program was carried out in the South Shore's Michigan City shops. In addition to the principal work of lengthening and strengthening underframes, and splicing in the additional car body length, the rebuilding program included the installation of new seating, fluorescent lighting, and a general interior modernization. The first two lengthened cars were completed in 1942, and by the end of 1946 the South Shore had placed 23 of the stretched-out cars in service. Not only did the lengthening program increase seating capacity by anywhere from 24 to 30 seats per car, but South Shore found that both car maintenance and operating costs per seat mile were significantly reduced.

Another important equipment improvement carried out during the war years was the installation of roller bearings on virtually all of the South Shore's rolling stock. By 1946 all of the railroad's locomotives and almost all of its passenger cars had been equipped.

Several improvements to the South Shore's physical plant, too, helped the railroad to successfully handle its heavy burden of wartime traffic. A new 3,500 foot siding installed at Birchim in 1941 helped to expedite freight traffic on the single track main line west of Michigan City. Between 1941 and 1946 the entire main line, except for track laid in paved streets, was reballasted with crushed rock. In 1942, 90-pound rail in Chicago Avenue at East Chicago, Indiana, was replaced with 100-pound stock, and a few years later several miles of main line track were relaid with heavier 112-pound rail. In 1944 work started on a complete reconstruction of the overhead catenary system between South Bend and Michigan City. Thus, in an unspectacular, continuing program of improvement and renovation, did the South Shore continue its evolution into a heavy duty railroad.

The South Shore's extraordinary traffic volume of the war years proved to be no short term bonanza. From a war's end peak of over six million passengers annually, passenger traffic fell off fairly sharply for the next several years, finally stabilizing from 1950 onward at an annual level of four to four and one-half million — a good million passengers a year above the South Shore's 3.2 million passenger pre-war peak year of 1929.

The decline in passenger revenues, however, was more than offset by the South Shore's continued growth as a freight carrier. From a war-time level of just over two million dollars annually, South Shore's freight income increased rapidly in the post-war period, reaching a level of close to $3.5 million by 1950. From a 1946 level of slightly over six million dollars, the South Shore's gross revenues grew steadily, passing the seven million mark for the first time in 1951.

The South Shore's passenger car lengthening program was continued after the war. By 1951 a total of 36 cars had been rebuilt. With several exceptions, all of the cars lengthened after 1946 were also equipped with air conditioning and fitted with lengthened "picture" windows. A number of the wartime rebuilds were also returned to the Michigan City shops during 1949-50 for similar treatment. The installation of air conditioning and new windows, together with the new seating and interior im-

A continuing program of maintenance and improvement provided the modern South Shore with track and roadbed of exceptionally high standards. This maintenance of way crew was resurfacing track east of Gary after placement of a new lift of crushed stone ballast in the summer of 1963.—WILLIAM D. MIDDLETON

In a setting that has changed but little in a half century, South Shore rails slice across the back yards of Hammond, Indiana. — ROBERT HEGGE (OPPOSITE PAGE) Although extensively rebuilt and enlarged over the years, this station at Gary has served South Shore passengers ever since the railway opened in 1908. Chicago-South Bend train No. 9 is about to depart on a June day in 1966. —WILLIAM D. MIDDLETON

In a post-war continuation of the South Shore's car lengthening and modernization program a total of 18 cars received air conditioning and picture windows. All three cars in this eastbound train, shown in a publicity photograph taken at Shadyside, Indiana, about 1949, had received the full lengthening and modernization program. The lead car was equipped with an experimental radio-telephone installation.—
COURTESY OF TRAINS MAGAZINE

South Shore freight traffic increased enormously under Insull management. Baldwin-Westinghouse locomotive No. 1007 is shown with a six-car freight at Hegewisch, Illinois.—LOUIS F. GERARD COLLECTION

Beverley Shores, another popular stop in the Dunes area got a handsome "Insull Spanish" style station during the late 1920's. Combine No. 109 headed a westbound train at the Shores during the early 1950's.—MWEH COLLECTION

Tremont station, midway between Gary and Michigan City, is South Shore's principal stop for traffic to the Indiana Dunes area of Lake Michigan.—WALLACE W. ABBEY

Three massive 273-ton locomotives added to the South Shore roster in 1949 provided the railroad with freight motive power comparable to that of a trunk line electrification. Originally built for the U.S.S.R., the three "Little Joe's" were among the largest electric engines ever built. No. 803 heads eastbound tonnage out of Burnham Yard.—MWEH COLLECTION (BELOW) After a quarter century of hauling New York Central trains between Grand Central Terminal and Harmon, seven of the Central's R-2 class electric locomotives were rebuilt by South Shore for freight service. Two are shown about to depart from Burnham Yard with an eastbound train.—WILLIAM D. MIDDLETON

The bleakness of winter surrounds an eastbound South Shore train at Hudson Lake, Indiana. Two rebuilt and lengthened Insull-era cars are trailed by a former Indiana Railroad RPO-combine used as an express trailer.—MWEH COLLECTION

provements and a general exterior restyling carried out under the post-war rebuilding program, provided South Shore with passenger equipment that was virtually the equal in both appearance and standards of passenger comfort to the latest post-war steam railroad equipment being operated in comparable service. By 1951 a total of 18 cars — nearly a third of the South Shore passenger car fleet and a sufficient number to operate all of the railroad's long haul schedules — had received the full modernization program.

During a period of little more than a decade following the end of the war, the South Shore carried out an upgrading of its freight motive power roster that almost entirely displaced the heavy steeple cab units of the 1920's with a fleet of massive locomotives that were typical of main line electrification practice. In 1949 three 273-ton, 2-D+D-2 locomotives, originally destined for the Soviet Union, were purchased from the General Electric Company and re-

built in the South Shore's Michigan City shops. Between 1955 and 1958 six 140-ton, C+C units purchased secondhand from the New York Central were extensively rebuilt by the Michigan City shops for South Shore service. Subsequently, a majority of the South Shore's lighter steeple cab units were taken out of service and sold for scrap.

Steady improvement to the South Shore's physical plant, too, continued in the post-war years. During the late 1940's South Shore installed a complete system-wide VHF radio installation — one of the first on any railroad. As early as 1937 South Shore had been one of the first railroad's to experiment with the use of butt pressure welded rail, and by 1950 the railroad had begun the regular use of welded rail for its normal replacement program, placing as many as five track miles every year. Bridges were strengthened to support the higher axle loadings of the line's heavier locomotives and high capacity modern freight cars.

The operation of heavy freight trains and frequent passenger service through congested traffic on Chicago Avenue in East Chicago, Indiana, represented a problem of long standing for South Shore until construction of the East Chicago bypass route in 1956. Until then, long freight trains represented an incongruous sight on the busy thoroughfare. Locomotive No. 803 is shown with a westbound train at the Indiana Harbor Canal and Indiana Harbor Belt Railroad crossing on Chicago Avenue.—o. f. LEE COLLECTION

During the mid-1950's the South Shore Line carried out what was easily its greatest single line improvement project since the Insull era of the 1920's — the construction of a two and one-half million dollar, five-mile relocation of the railroad's main line at East Chicago, Indiana.

For more than 30 years the operation of South Shore trains through Chicago Avenue, the principal east-west business street in East Chicago, had represented a source of irritation to local residents and of serious delays to the railroad's trains. Indeed, as early as 1927 the South Shore's Insull management had recognized the problem as one that required prompt solution. "It is absolutely necessary for us to get off Chicago Avenue . . ." said South Shore vice president Charles W. Chase at the time.

Real estate for an East Chicago bypass line on private right-of-way was purchased during 1927. Plans for construction of the new double track line and a new East Chicago station, to be completed by the end of 1928, were announced the following August. Approval for construction of the bypass was obtained from the Indiana Public Service Commission, but the East Chicago City Council, unhappy with the excessive number of grade crossings planned for the line, managed to block a start of the work by contesting the authority of the Com-

mission to grant a permit to construct tracks over city streets and alleys. The South Shore successfully appealed the action all the way to the Indiana Supreme Court, but it was 1930 before the legal problems had been cleared up and the railroad finally had approval to proceed with construction. By this time the Depression had arrived, and the South Shore was no longer in a position to carry out a substantial line relocation or any other major improvements.

By the early 1950's the Chicago Avenue problem had become intolerable. A 1952 traffic check on the busy thoroughfare, for example, showed that during a typical 16-hour weekday period a bus, truck, auto, or South Shore train used the street every four and a half seconds on the average. On the South Shore line through East Chicago there were 15 separate railroad grade crossings with a total of 27 tracks, and 22 separate street crossings, including six in the two miles of Chicago Avenue trackage with traffic lights which South Shore trains were required to observe.

At almost the same time that the South Shore Line was laying plans to proceed with construction of the long-planned project, the Indiana Toll Road Commission was seeking an economic route through the same area for its east-west toll highway across Northern Indi-

A few years before World War II coach No. 34 headed a two-car train across the Indiana Habor Canal and Indiana Harbor Belt crossing in East Chicago's Chicago Avenue. Traffic congestion in the busy thoroughfare represented an aggravation to South Shore operations of over three decades standing before it was finally eliminated by completion of the East Chicago bypass in 1956. — WILLIAM C. JANSSEN

Just before opening of the East Chicago bypass in 1956 a South Shore ballast sweeper puts finishing touches on new track near the Indianapolis Avenue station.—STEPHEN D. MAGUIRE

No. 50, a former Arlington & Fairfax Electric Railway road-rail bus, was used to install overhead insulators during construction of the East Chicago bypass. (BELOW) A day before regular operation over the East Chicago bypass began on September 16, 1956, only the final connections of track and overhead catenary remained to be completed in this view at the eastern end of the bypass, just west of the Elgin, Joliet & Eastern overcrossing at Cavanaugh. The track at left led to the original route through East Chicago.—BOTH STEPHEN D. MAGUIRE

ana. The Commission proposed that they and the South Shore join in joint construction of their two routes through East Chicago utilizing the right-of-way already acquired by the railroad, an arrangement that was to prove mutually advantageous.

Under the agreement between the toll road commission and South Shore, 110 acres of railroad-owned land were deeded to the Commission. In return, the Commission agreed to build an elevated, five-mile right-of-way through East Chicago, including all necessary bridges, for the joint use of the toll highway and the South Shore. In addition, the South Shore was paid some $850,000 in cash. With a further investment of only two and one-half million dollars for track, power, signal, and station facilities, the South Shore was able to complete the construction of a superb high speed, entirely grade separated, electric line that would permit a major improvement to the railroad's freight and passenger service.

Actual construction work started in 1954 and the new line was completed and placed in operation in the fall of 1956. The elevated line was built almost entirely on an embankment, which required nearly a million cubic yards of pumped sand fill. A total of 12 steel bridges, with a combined length of 4,180 feet, was required to carry the line over streets, other rail-

Just before operation began over the new bypass line, a South Shore line crew completed the necessary connections in the overhead catenary system at the eastern end of the bypass. The line train included a former Buffalo Creek Railway diesel switcher No. 42, line car No. 1100, and a wire car. The view above shows the wire gang tightening the trolley wire splicers, suspensions, and trolley wire ears.—BOTH STEPHEN D. MAGUIRE

On the day before regular operation began over the East Chicago bypass this special train, headed by coach No. 27, carried an inspection party of railroad officials and guests over the new route. The eastbound three-car special is shown at the eastern end of the bypass, with the original route visible at the right. — BODIE PHOTOGRAPHER, COURTESY OF RAILROAD MAGAZINE In the close-up at the left, mayors and city officials from East Chicago, Hammond, and Gary are flanked by South Shore president Jay Samuel Hartt (waving at left) and vice president and general manager Charles H. Jones at the right. —STEPHEN D. MAGUIRE (OPPOSITE PAGE) The joint South Shore bypass and Indiana Toll Road construction through East Chicago, Indiana, affords an excellent example of a modern transportation artery. A two-car westbound train is shown on the "super railroad" bypass near Cavanaugh in 1958. The property to the right of the Toll Road was part of the railroad's South Shore Industrial District developed in conjunction with the new line.—ARA MESROBIAN

roads, and the Grand Calumet River. Track was constructed with welded 115 pound rail, laid on creosoted ties with rubber tie pads and double shoulder plates, and founded in crushed stone ballast. Maximum curvature on the line was limited to 2.5 degrees and track was superelevated to permit 60 m.p.h. speeds. A compound catenary overhead system was supported by catenary bridges built of rolled steel sections spaced at 300 feet. A new substation was built at Parrish Avenue, about midway in the new line. Four passenger stops on the old line were replaced by a single new East Chicago station at Indianapolis Avenue. A parking lot adjacent to the station provided space for 600 commuter automobiles, and a reversible escalator carried passengers to and from the elevated station platform.

The new bypass was opened to regular traffic on September 16, 1956. Not only was the South Shore able to cut about ten minutes from passenger train running times through East Chicago, but the freedom from traffic delays permitted an increase in on-time performance from about 92 percent to 98 percent of all passenger trains. Even more time was saved by freight trains, which were able to save 15 to 20 minutes over the timings through East Chicago via the original route.

Even before construction of the East Chicago bypass had started, the freight-conscious South Shore had recognized an opportunity in the project totally apart from the primary benefit of improving freight and passenger train operating conditions. Some 270 acres of undeveloped real estate adjacent to the route

A latticework of steel girders of the Calumet River bridge just east of Kensington is framed in the front window of Gary-Chicago train No. 110. — WILLIAM D. MIDDLETON (BELOW) Four cars of eastbound South Shore commuters roll down the long slope from the Ford City overcrossing into Hegewisch station in June 1968. (OPPOSITE PAGE) A South Shore M.U. train westbound at high speed, the graceful curve of the compound catenary, and the latticework of high tension transmission towers along the East Chicago bypass combine in a dramatic portrayal of electric energy at work.—BOTH JOHN GRUBER

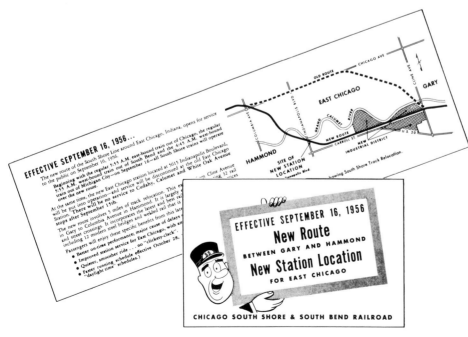

A four-car westbound train descends from the elevated East Chicago bypass to rejoin the original South Shore alignment at Calumet Avenue in Hammond.—JOHN GRUBER (UPPER RIGHT) A modern station at Indianapolis Avenue on the new bypass replaced four passenger stops on the old route through the city. Michigan City-Chicago train No. 214 slows for a passenger stop at Indianapolis Avenue in 1964.—WILLIAM D. MIDDLETON (RIGHT) Paced from the parallel Indiana Toll Road, a three-car South Shore train races eastward on the East Chicago bypass in a 1968 scene of pantograph and catenary action. —JOHN GRUBER On the opposite page, one of the folders issued by South Shore to acquaint the riding public with the new bypass location and station changes.—DONALD DUKE COLLECTION

In a vivid portrayal of high speed electric railroading, westbound South Shore M.U.'s race toward Chicago along the "super railroad" track of the East Chicago bypass.—JOUN GRUBER

of the new line and southeast of the central business district of East Chicago were acquired by South Shore for industrial development purposes. Even before the new bypass was opened, several carload freight generating industries were under construction in the railroad's South Shore Industrial District.

Despite the benefits of the new East Chicago line, however, the South Shore was headed for a few bumpy years during the late 1950's. Although gross revenues remained relatively stable, an upward trend in operating costs dropped South Shore net income (before taxes) from more than $560,000 in 1956 to a deficit of almost $84,000 in 1958. By the end of 1960 the annual deficit had reached more than $175,000.

A vigorous cost reduction and traffic expansion program launched by new president and general manager William P. Coliton, who took office early in 1961, quickly set things right again. Internal reorganization and a cut in the size of the payroll helped generate modest savings, and increased mechanization permitted a reduction in maintenance of way costs. Several unprofitable operations were dropped. A switch from railroad-operated restaurants to coin concessions in stations converted a substantial an-

In this scene, a South Shore train rolls westbound at high speed, the graceful curve of the compound catenary, and the latticework of high tension transmission towers along the East Chicago bypass combine to give the photograph the look of high speed electric railroading in full action.—JOHN GRUBER

In a busy moment during an afternoon rush hour in 1968, car No. 108 in the view above, heads an eastbound passenger run past Burnham Yard, just across the state line from Hammond, Indiana. Two former New York Central R-2 electrics and a "Little Joe" are ready to head eastbound tonnage out of the yard. The passenger train is running on the westbound main in order to clear a long coal train. (LEFT) A welcome addition to South Shore on-line industries during the early 1960's was Northern Indiana Public Service Company's Bailly Generating Station, which will eventually consume 1,700,000 tons of South Shore delivered coal annually. "Little Joe" No. 802 accelerated out of Burnham Yard in 1968 with a Bailly-bound unit train of southern Indiana soft coal.—BOTH JOHN GRUBER

Until the railroad moved its passenger terminal to the western edge of South Bend in 1970, South Shore trains terminated their runs in typical interurban fashion in the middle of South Bend's LaSalle Avenue, opposite a convenient downtown station on the corner of La Salle and Michigan Street. Packages and express are important as well as passengers to South Shore. In the scene below, package freight is unloaded from the baggage trailer of a second section of Chicago-South Bend limited train No. 15.—WILLIAM D. MIDDLETON At the left, one of the many brochures published to inform the small shipper about the convenience and "on time" performance of South Shore parcel delivery.—DONALD DUKE COLLECTION

Another means of promoting parcel and express service was the colorful ink blotters handed out by South Shore. At the right are two fine examples of this well executed promotion. — DONALD DUKE COLLECTION (BELOW) Parcels and passengers are loaded aboard a South Bend-Chicago train in 11th Street at Michigan City in 1955. —ARA MESROBIAN

With one hand on the controller and the other on the air horn, the motorman of South Bend Limited train No. 13 worried his way through East Chicago street traffic in the summer of 1955. A year later completion of the new East Chicago bypass eliminated this worrisome part of the trip to South Bend. (BELOW) At South Bend, passengers board the single car of Chicago Limited train No. 22 in the summer of 1955.—BOTH WILLIAM D. MIDDLETON

Engulfed in heavy downtown South Bend traffic a two-car train loaded for a Chicago run in the fall of 1969.—DUANE HALL FROM CHICAGO SUN-TIMES

A South Shore motorman waits patiently as he glances along his train of orange and maroon interurban cars for the highball that will begin his westbound trip from South Bend. —FRED SCHNEIDER

Under the singing overhead trolley wire, a pair of South Shore interurbans roll down La Salle Avenue of South Bend on a tranquil Sunday afternoon.—GORDON LLOYD

In a setting that has doubtless changed but little from the days of alternating current catenary and the big wood Niles cars of the old Lake Shore, two modernized South Shore interurbans kick up a cloud of dust as they rumble down an unpaved South Bend street at Linden School on the way to Chicago in the summer of 1966.—ARA MESROBIAN

After completing their runs, South Shore trains are readied for the return trip to Chicago in the railroad's South Bend storage yard a few blocks beyond the downtown station. Interurban car No. 104 headed out of the yard for a run to Chicago as train No. 20 in March 1945 while trackmen rebuilt the yard.—C. W. JERNSTROM At the left, combine No. 108 is run through the yard's car washer in April 1946. — JOHN F. HORAN FROM TRAINS MAGAZINE (BELOW) A 1936 scene of the South Bend yard showing interurban cars in storage in the yard and on the street after their arrival from Chicago.— MWEH COLLECTION On the opposite page, the last South Shore steeple cab locomotives in regular service were two of the road's 1930 General Electric units. Here, they head a work train at Wilson, Indiana, in 1964 as two-car South Bend-Chicago train No. 20 flashes by at speed on the westbound main.—WILLIAM D. MIDDLETON

Although normally used only for freight service, South Shore's three "Little Joe" locomotives, with a rating of over 5,000 h.p. and geared for a maximum speed of 68 m.p.h. were well adopted to occasional special movements such as this 10-car Illinois Central picnic train. The train of arch-roofed Harriman coaches was eastbound at the Pennsylvania-Wabash (now Penn Central and Norfolk & Western) overcrossing just west of Gary. (BELOW) The same train is seen eastbound at Wagner siding, east of Gary.—BOTH MWEH COLLECTION

nual loss to a handsome profit. The South Shore's remaining motor coach service between Michigan City and Benton Harbor, which lost nearly $33,000 in 1961, was sold early in 1963.

Passenger schedule reductions late in 1961 helped to cut operating costs in line with a downward trend in traffic, and a 1962 fare increase further helped to narrow the gap between passenger revenues and costs. A traffic department reorganization and formation of a new industrial development department both contributed to a substantial increase in freight revenues.

By the end of 1961 South Shore was back in the black with a slightly better than break-even net profit, and by 1964 the annual net, before taxes, was approaching $400,000, the company's best showing in over a decade.

At the heart of the South Shore's difficulties of the late 1950's, and a trouble source that was only temporarily set aside by the corrective measures of the Coliton administration, was what may be referred to simply as the "passenger problem." In common with almost every other North American railroad that derived a significant portion of its income from the carriage of passengers, the South Shore since the end of World War II had been caught in the grip of rising labor and operating costs, which were nowhere near offset by increases in passenger fares. On a fully distributed cost basis the South Shore had been running passenger trains at a loss since the beginning of the 1950's, and the annual passenger deficit had climbed as high as $719,000 in 1958.

Even apart from the problem of passenger deficit, there seemed to be ample reason to doubt that there was any future at all for South Shore passenger business. After holding at a relatively steady level for a number of years, South Shore passenger traffic began a long term decline in the mid-1950's. Completion of the Indiana Toll Road in 1956, and of the Dan Ryan Expressway in 1962, which gave motorists direct freeway access to the Chicago Loop, both brought sharp drops in South Shore's daily passenger count. From a 1955 level of over 4,440,000, revenue passengers declined to a 1965 total of just over 3,135,000 — a drop of

Just west of Gary, Indiana, a gauntlet track carries South Shore trains through a truss bridge crossing over the Penn Central and Norfolk & Western railroads. Lengthened and modernized cars thunder the South Bend-Chicago train No. 20 upgrade toward the bridge.—WILLIAM D. MIDDLETON

Led by combine No. 103, a two-car South Bend Limited sweeps around a curve on the west side of Michigan City in May 1968. — JOHN GRUBER

almost 30 percent in only a decade. Even more abrupt than this general decline was the drastic fall-off in the South Shore's long-haul passengers, the railroad's most profitable passenger business. Between 1950 and 1965, for example, traffic in and out of South Bend declined by almost two thirds. Increasingly, the railroad's passenger business was dominated by commuter traffic between Chicago and the close-in stations west of Gary. By the mid-1960's some 85 percent of the South Shore's passenger business was concentrated on the line west of Gary.

Reflecting the decline in its long-haul traffic, the railroad in 1970 moved its South Bend terminal to a new location near the Bendix plant on the west side of the city, eliminating the costs and problems of some two miles of passenger train operation through city streets, as well as the costly maintenance requirement for over a mile of passenger-only track located in city streets. Both the terminal building at Michigan and La Salle and the South Bend terminal yard property were sold.

Despite the long-term decline of recent years, however, continuing industrial development and population growth along the south shore of Lake Michigan seemed to offer good long range prospects for a stabilized or even expanded South Shore commuter traffic between Chicago and points perhaps as far east as Michigan City. Indeed, after a decade of decline, the railroad's passenger volume had begun to show a modest annual growth after 1965.

Thus far, the South Shore had kept the problem of passenger deficit under control by means of a combination of service curtailments and fare increases. In the long run, of course, such measures would prove self-defeating. In any case, under the limitations imposed by existing equipment and operating conditions, and a fare level the traffic would bear, elimination of the passenger deficit remained beyond the South Shore's reach. Since overcoming the losses of the early 1960's, the railroad had generally managed to balance the loss of passenger revenue with profits from its freight traffic.

110

In a scene that recalls the typical midwestern interurban, Chicago-bound South Shore combine No. 100 accelerates away from a station stop at Hudson Lake, Indiana, on a warm day in 1966.—ARA MESROBIAN

Gary represents both the South Shore's most important intermediate stop and the eastern end of its heaviest commuter district. Commuters cluster on the high-level platform as train No. 10, a morning South Bend-Chicago schedule, brakes to a stop at Gary. In the view above, a trainman acknowledges a highball as a Gary-Chicago train is ready for departure from Gary.—BOTH WILLIAM D. MIDDLETON (OPPOSITE PAGE) At Hegewisch, a motorman looks back expectantly for the conductor's highball.—JOHN GRUBER At the right, the train conductor on South Bend train No. 17 picks up tickets on the way out of Chicago.—WILLIAM D. MIDDLETON Crowded with holiday traffic, eight-car Chicago train No 16 rolls past Burnham Yard.—WILLIAM C. JANSSEN

Despite a wet, heavy snow that clings wherever it falls, the South Shore trains are running. Coach No. 33 leads a two-car train along the streets of Michigan City. (BELOW) Interurbans in the yard at South Bend were plastered with snow and ice after arriving from Chicago during a bitter 1954 storm.— BOTH MWEH COLLECTION

By the mid-1960's another aspect of South Shore's passenger problem — its aging equipment fleet — was beginning to assume increasingly critical proportions. Despite modernization and an extremely high standard of maintenance over the years, the Insull era passenger cars — now 40 years or more old — were becoming increasingly costly to keep in operation. In 1967, for example, South Shore spent $670,000 on the maintenance of its 64 passenger cars. Even apart from the need to reduce maintenance costs with modern equipment, South Shore badly needed the operating cost savings, the increased earning potential, and the greater passenger comfort that it could get from modern lightweight, high performance, low maintenance equipment. The acquisition of such equipment, unfortunately, was no more within the South Shore's means than was elimination of the passenger deficit.

The solution to the twin horns of the South Shore passenger dilemma, if there was going to be one other than ultimate abandonment of passenger operation, seemed to lie in the eventual formation of some sort of public body through which Federal funds under the Urban Mass Transportation Act of 1964 could be loaned for the purchase of new equipment, and to which the South Shore could look for some sort of passenger subsidy. As the South Shore began its seventh decade of operation, the railroad was working with the newly-formed Lake-Porter County Regional Transportation and Planning Commission toward such a plan which, if successful, might place a fleet of new equipment on South Shore rails by the early 1970's.

Aside from the nagging passenger problem, South Shore has been doing quite well throughout most of the 1960's. Since the early 1960's the railroad had been profiting from a major industrial boom centering around the Burns Ditch area, midway between Gary and Michigan City. First on the scene was Midwest Steel Corporation, which opened a fully integrated steel plant at Burns Ditch in 1961. Late in 1964 Bethlehem Steel Corporation completed a $350 million Burns Harbor steel rolling and finishing plant which was planned for an eventual capa-

Bethlehem Steel's huge Burns Harbor plant was still under construction in the summer of 1964 as Chicago Limited No. 20 roared past on a long stretch of double track at Wilson. (BELOW) South Shore's No. 1100 represented the very last word in electric railway line cars. The car was rebuilt from a former Indiana Railroad Railway Post Office unit in 1947. In this scene, No. 1100 is shown engaged in overhead catenary maintenance in 1964 near the site of Bethlehem Steel's new Burns Harbor plant.—WILLIAM D. MIDDLETON

Former Great Northern and Minneapolis & St. Louis executive William P. Coliton guided the South Shore Line through financial difficulties as president from 1961 until 1966.—BACHRACH PHOTO FROM CSS&SB (RIGHT) Chicago business executive James McCahey, Jr., who joined the South Shore as general manager in 1965 and succeeded William P. Coliton as president in 1966, faces the formidable task of finding answers to the South Shore's problems of passenger deficits and replacement of its aging equipment.—MOFFETT STUDIO FROM CSS&SB

city of over two million tons annually. Although both plants were served exclusively by the New York Central, the South Shore gained substantial freight traffic from the various satellite industries that located in the Burns Harbor area to serve the steel mills.

Of much more direct benefit to South Shore was the 183,000 k.w. Bailly Generating Station completed by the Northern Indiana Public Service Company late in 1962 on a site adjacent to that of Bethlehem Steel. Exclusively served by the South Shore Line, the Bailly plant initially consumed 400,000 tons of rail-hauled coal a year. Originating in southern Indiana mines, the traffic moved over four different railroads in 100-car unit trains, with South Shore electric power handling the last leg of the journey from Burnham Yard to the Bailly plant. A new 414,-000 k.w. generating unit for the Bailly plant was completed during 1968, by which time coal tonnage being delivered by South Shore had increased to a million tons annually. Ultimately, South Shore expected to be moving a

coal traffic of 1,700,000 tons a year into the huge plant.

Still further industrial expansion for the Burns Harbor area was forecast as a result of the planned construction by the State of Indiana of a deep water Lake Michigan harbor which would give the area — and South Shore — direct access to St. Lawrence Seaway traffic. Initial construction work for the harbor was started in 1966.

During the early 1960's the growing trend toward large scale railroad mergers became the source of increasing concern to South Shore management. The several pending mergers among South Shore connections — Baltimore & Ohio-Chesapeake & Ohio, Pennsy-N.Y.C., and Nickel Plate and Wabash into Norfolk & Western — threatened South Shore with a much more disadvantageous competitive situation. Fully 70 percent of South Shore's freight traffic was overhead or "bridge" traffic, both originating and terminating on other lines, and much of it could well be lost as a result of marriages

Headed by lengthened combine No. 102, a westbound South Bend-Chicago train rolls downgrade past Smith stop, a few miles east of Tee Lake, Indiana, in June 1947. This photo shows the rural aspect of portions of the South Shore Line.—WILLIAM C. JANSSEN

The interurban tradition still lingers on the South Shore at Michigan City. As children watch from a front stoop, a South Shore Limited rumbles down 11th Street a few blocks east of the railroad's Michigan City station in the summer of 1964.—WILLIAM D. MIDDLETON

For a few moments traffic was snarled in Michigan City's 11th Street as a three-car train led by lengthened Pullman-built combine No. 100 paused for a station stop.—WILLIAM C. JANSSEN (LEFT) A trainman dons his gloves during a station stop at Hammond, Indiana.—JOHN GRUBER

Eastbound for South Bend, a long train leaves Michigan City street trackage at the Michigan Street stop.—DONALD DUKE COLLECTION (BELOW) On a warm tranquil day during May 1968, a train led by No. 110 is passed by another passenger at Michigan City.—JOHN GRUBER

In this rural South Shore scene, a two-car Chicago train headed by coach No. 22 heads out of the Tremont siding during the early 1950's.—ARA MESROBIAN

East of Gary, South Bend-Chicago train No. 22 is framed in heavy summer foliage as the two-car limited clears the Baltimore & Ohio overpass at Miller in July 1963.— WILLIAM D. MIDDLETON

Gary after dark . . . South Bend train No. 35 is ready to roll at the left, while the Post Office truck picks up mail at the right.— WILLIAM D. MIDDLETON

between some of its connections. Independence was proving to have other disadvantages, too. Largely because of South Shore's inability to guarantee a large car supply, Bethelehem Steel refused to grant the electric line access to its Burns Harbor plant so long as it remained an independent road. Thus, from about 1960 onward, South Shore was actively seeking an advantageous affiliation with a large connecting trunk line.

Previously, South Shore's deficit passenger operation had tended to discourage any merger ambitions on the part of other systems. By the early 1960's, however, the massive industrial development in the Burns Harbor area, a choice traffic plum South Shore shared only with the New York Central, suddenly made the electric line a much more eligible merger partner.

Doubtless beguiled by the Burns Harbor activity, as well as other South Shore industrial connections, the neighboring Monon moved to acquire a substantial block of South Shore stock, and early in 1964 asked for representation on the electric line's board and a merger study. Concluding that it could do better than a Monon tie-up, South Shore successfully fended off the Monon's bid for control.

The next trunk line to make a bid for South Shore was the Chesapeake & Ohio, a move which was much more welcome to South Shore. Early in 1965 C&O, with the South Shore's blessing, applied to the Interstate Commerce Commission for permission to acquire South Shore control. The application was approved late in 1966, and on January 3, 1967, C&O assumed control of the electric line, subsequently acquiring ownership of some 94 percent of the South Shore's outstanding stock shares.

In balance then, the end of the 1960's found the South Shore Line doing fairly well. The railroad now enjoyed all the advantages of ownership by a large and powerful trunk line. Freight business was good and prospects for future growth were bright indeed. Gross revenues, which by 1968 were running in excess of eight million dollars a year, were at the highest level in the railroad's entire history. There remained, of course, the passenger problem to be dealt with. If a solution was not yet in hand, there was at least room for cautious optimism that one was going to be found short of passenger service abandonment. Certainly in its 60 years the adroit South Shore had successfully overcome other crises of equal gravity.

As it began its seventh decade of service, then, the South Shore Line could face the future with a high level of confidence. Once a typical interurban, the railroad had managed to transform itself into a heavy electric railroad already fully integrated into the North American railway network. The South Shore's passenger trains had become a vital component of the system of suburban railroads that moved thousands of Chicago-area commuters between home and workplace every workday, and its busy freight trains were a no less important transportation resource for the business and industry of northwestern Indiana.

4

TO THE LOOP
ON
ILLINOIS CENTRAL

EVER SINCE the completion of its entire main line between South Bend and Pullman in 1909, the South Shore has depended upon the suburban lines of the Illinois Central Railroad to transport its passengers into the heart of Chicago.

Initially, South Shore passengers transferred to IC suburban trains at Pullman. Although South Shore schedules were coordinated with those of the IC trains, passengers were obliged to utilize an overhead footbridge to get across the IC main line tracks between the South Shore platforms and those of the suburban trains, and the steam powered IC trains were slow and dirty. Samuel Insull, Jr., later described this means of entrance into Chicago as "fiendish," and estimated that the transfer arrangement was costing the South Shore at least 50 percent of the potential business, an observation that is well substantiated by the traffic results following the installation of through service to the Loop in 1926.

The transfer arrangement was somewhat improved in 1911, when completion of a new interlocking plant at Kensington permitted the South Shore trains to cross over the IC main line to the same platforms used by the suburban trains. A much more important improvement was made the following year, when the two railroads agreed to operate a number of through coaches between South Shore Line

On the right, a train of orange and maroon South Shore M.U.'s is switched in the South Shore's terminal tracks at Chicago's Randolph Station in 1963. The landmark Prudential Building was constructed on air rights over the Illinois Central terminal during the 1950's. (OPPOSITE PAGE) Its journey over Illinois Central suburban rails completed, a four-car South Bend Limited has just crossed over the IC main line at Kensington. From this point to the Indiana border, South Shore trains travel over the Kensington & Eastern Railroad, a connection with the South Shore completed by IC in 1909 and leased by the electric line ever since.—BOTH WILLIAM D. MIDDLETON

125

Until the Illinois Central catenary was energized in 1926 South Shore passengers completed their journey to the Loop in Illinois Central suburban trains like this. The train of steel and aluminum coaches, which still operate as trailers with IC's M.U. cars, date this view of a northbound train to early 1920's.—ILLINOIS CENTRAL RAILROAD

126

Outbound for South Bend, South Shore train No. 13 approaches the IC suburban platforms at Roosevelt Road. Beyond, the towering buildings of Chicago's prestigious Michigan Avenue establish a magnificent urban skyline.—WILLIAM D. MIDDLETON (BELOW) With coach No. 1 in the lead, a South Shore train stands at the high-level platforms in IC's Randolph Street Station in a view dating from the 1930's. The towering Prudential Building constructed over the station has since altered the backdrop to this scene.—CHARLES GOETHE COLLECTION

Framed by the steel latticework of a catenary bridge, against a backdrop of the towers of Michigan Avenue, the maroon and orange cars of South Shore's South Bend-Chicago train No. 12 pauses to discharge Loop commuters at IC's Roosevelt Road station. (BELOW) With ornate tower of architect Bradford L. Gilbert's 19th century Central Station in the background, South Shore's South Bend-Chicago train No. 6 accelerates away from the platforms at Roosevelt Road on the way into Van Buren and Randolph Street stations.—BOTH WILLIAM D. MIDDLETON

While a Chicago-bound Illinois Central suburban train pauses at the 43rd Street platforms, six-car South Bend Limited No. 16 roars past on non-stop trackage. The first stop beyond the Loop for South Shore trains is the Hyde Park station at 53rd Street.—MWEH COLLECTION (RIGHT) Racing toward Randolph Street on the outer "special" track reserved for non-stop trains, a four-car South Shore train was about to overtake an Illinois Central local in this 1956 view on the six-track right-of-way not far from the Loop.—WILLIAM D. MIDDLETON

A South Shore train glides into the platform stop at Woodlawn (63rd Street), just seven miles and 13 minutes from downtown Chicago. — FRED SCHNEIDER (BELOW) Four cars strong, a Michigan City-Chicago express thunders down Illinois Central rails toward the Chicago Loop. Brakes are beginning to grab at spinning steel wheels as the train slows for the Woodlawn station stop.—WILLIAM D. MIDDLETON

Bound for the Chicago Loop, four South Shore M.U.'s operating as South Bend-Chicago train No. 12 cross over the Illinois Central main line tracks at Kensington to join IC suburban rails for the run to Randolph Street Station. (BELOW) Eyeing the approaching air-conditioned South Shore coaches longingly in the heat of a Chicago summer, prospective passengers edge forward as South Bend Limited train No. 13 approaches its Kensington stop at 115th Street. — BOTH WILLIAM D. MIDDLETON

points and the IC's Randolph Street Suburban Station.

The true potential of South Shore passenger traffic, however, was never reached until 1926, when the new Insull management re-equipped and re-electrified the entire railroad to conform to the Illinois Central's new suburban electrification, and negotiated a contract with IC that permitted South Shore to operate all of its trains directly to Randolph Street Station in the Chicago Loop.

Access to the new IC electrification provided the South Shore Line with an entrance into Chicago over what ranks as perhaps the finest suburban railroad system anywhere in North America. The entire main line of the IC suburban system is fully grade separated from roads or other rail lines and is reserved exclusively for suburban traffic. At Kensington, where South Shore trains transfer to IC, the suburban main line expands to four tracks and at 50th Street, to six, to provide separate "local," "express," and "special" tracks in each direction. The 1,500 volt D.C. power is fed to suburban trains through a compound catenary overhead system supported by steel catenary bridges. Train movements are governed by electric interlocking plants and a four position color-light block signal system. Stations throughout the suburban system are provided with high-level platforms for rapid loading and unloading. Scheduled stops at a total of six stations on the IC suburban system permitted the South Shore Line to offer a service of unparalleled convenience to points on the South Side and in the Chicago Loop.

Without question, the South Shore's utilization of the superb Illinois Central suburban system provided the railroad with the finest entry to a major metropolitan area ever attained by any interurban, and provided the South Shore with a competitive advantage to which it owed its very survival as a passenger carrier.

Just arrived from South Bend at mid-morning in April 1998, westbound train 14 discharged its passengers at the South Shore platforms in Metra Electric's Randolph Street suburban station. —WILLIAM D. MIDDLETON

Against the background of an ever-changing Michigan Avenue skyline, the South Shore's eastbound train 107 accelerated out of the Randolph Street station on its way from Chicago to Michigan City on an April morning in 1998. —WILLIAM D. MIDDLETON

Running against the flow of morning rush-hour traffic, the South Shore's eastbound train 207 for Gary approached the stop at Metra Electric's Roosevelt Road station. Beyond, a magnificent Michigan Avenue skyline towered over the lakefront rail lines. —WILLIAM D. MIDDLETON

On a warm July morning in 1983, westbound train 208 had just crossed over the Illinois Central Gulf main line at the Kensington interlocking to approach the 115th Street station stop on ICG's suburban electric route into Chicago. The three-car train was a rush-hour schedule from Gary. —WILLIAM D. MIDDLETON

South Shore C-C locomotives Nos. 701 and 702, the first two of seven ex-New York Central R-2 electrics rebuilt by South Shore, stand in Burnham Yard after bringing tonnage up from the Illinois Central interchange at Kensington in 1964.—WILLIAM D. MIDDLETON

5

ELECTRIC FREIGHT

"THERE WAS one little thing done, whether by design or accident I do not know," related Samuel Insull, Jr. of the South Shore recently, "which was responsible for our being able to rehabilitate the line and place it on a profitable basis, and for the continuation of the line in operation today."

This "one little thing," according to Insull, was the fact that the original builders of the Chicago, Lake Shore & South Bend Railway had laid out the entire line without the sharp curves to follow city streets that were customary with most interurbans. Instead, relates Insull, "Whenever they came to a corner the original projectors of the line bought the corner lots and flattened out the curve enough so that trains composed of standard railroad freight cars could negotiate the whole line from one end to the other. This was the key to the whole thing."

It is a curious paradox in its history that the South Shore Line, which was one of the few interurbans constructed to standards that would readily permit carload freight operation, and which today owes its very survival to such traffic, never, at the time of its opening, had any intention of engaging in the carload freight business. It was the opinion, in fact, of Frank H. Monks, one of several consulting engineers who studied the traffic potential of the planned interurban, that the road was one that would not benefit from freight operations aside from the sort of freight and express matter that could be carried aboard the passenger trains, for which Monks recommended the purchase of equipment with large baggage compartments.

The South Shore, then, despite the heavy industrial activity in its territory, was built without any strategically located sidings or freight stations, and no effort was made to secure on-line industries. For the first years of its existence, the South Shore contented itself with developing a modest traffic in package freight and express carried aboard the company's regular trains.

Virtually identical to the Chicago, Lake Shore & South Bend's own box cab freight locomotives, Inland Empire 72-ton locomotive No. 706 was operated in leased service on the South Shore around 1926. In this view No. 706 is shown at Fraser siding with a westbound freight in 1926.—C. E. HEDSTROM COLLECTION

The discouraging early financial performance of the road, however, caused South Shore management to take a second look at the possibilities for developing a profitable carload freight business, and on August 1, 1916, regular freight service between South Bend and Chicago was inaugurated with the 5:00 p.m. departure from South Bend of a motor car and one standard freight car. A box car set off the track at Cummins Siding in South Bend was the South Shore's first freight station.

After trial of a 6,600 volt A.C. Baldwin-Westinghouse locomotive leased from the Inland Empire system in the state of Washington, the South Shore ordered two similiar locomotives from Baldwin-Westinghouse. Placed in operation during October 1916, the two box cab type locomotives were considerably heavier and more powerful than most interurban railway freight locomotives. Weighing 72 tons fully equipped, each of the locomotives was powered by four 170 h.p. A.C. motors and was capable of exerting an hourly tractive effort of 20,800 pounds, with a continuous tractive effort rating of 13,600 pounds. Control systems permitted operation of the two locomotives in multiple unit when necessary.

Team tracks were installed at suitable locations along the entire road, and sites were acquired in nine principal cities and towns on the railway for the construction of freight houses. Until the new freight houses were completed during 1917, the road limited its freight business to carload traffic only. An interchange agreement with the always-friendly Illinois Central at Kensington gave the interurban access to points throughout the Chicago area as well as those on the IC system. Another interchange was established with the Elgin, Joliet & Eastern at Goff Junction in Gary, providing access to the steel mills and other heavy industries located on the Chicago Outer Belt. Joint tariffs were established with some 90 steam roads, and the South Shore became a member of the American Railway Association.

Except for switching, South Shore freight service was operated almost entirely at night. Freight cars loaded by 6 p.m. in Chicago were set out by the Illinois Central at Kensington before 1 a.m. and delivered anywhere on the South Shore before 8 a.m. the next morning. A similar westbound service was offered. A comparable overnight delivery for LCL traffic between Chicago and South Shore points was operated in conjunction with the IC. An even faster service was available to and from Chicago points by means of a direct connection with a drayage firm at Kensington. A few years later the South Shore established a popular twice-weekly refrigerator car service for perishable traffic.

During its first few years the South Shore's freight service was a moderate success. Additional interchange points were established with the Pullman Railroad at Kensington, with the Chicago & Calumet River Railroad at Hegewisch, with the Indiana Harbor Belt at East

Chicago, with the Lake Erie & Western at Michigan City, and with the Chicago, South Bend & Northern Indiana Railway at New Carlisle. Direct service was established to several major industries at South Bend, including the Oliver plow works, the Studebaker plants, and the Singer sewing machine works. Several on-line sand and gravel pits contributed a large business in construction materials.

From a level of less than $5,000 annually from the package freight service previously operated, the railway's freight revenues reached some $27,000 in 1917, the first full year of carload freight operation, and continued a steady growth thereafter. Initially, no more than four or five cars each way were handled by the nightly freights, but within a few years trains of 25 cars or more were regularly being handled. In 1921 almost 6,500 carloads were interchanged with the Illinois Central alone.

Despite its moderate growth, the South Shore's freight traffic reached nowhere near the volume that was potentially available in the railway's heavily industrialized territory, and freight revenues were never sufficient to convert the Chicago, Lake Shore & South Bend into a profitable venture. The barrier to real success in the South Shore's attempt to develop a substantial carload business was the implacable refusal of the majority of its potential steam railroad connections to have anything at all to do with any electric line. As a consequence, the South Shore was denied the interchanges that would give it access to the majority of industries in its territory, and was unable to participate in any significant amount of long-haul traffic. What traffic it was able to develop was largely confined to on-line movements, and traffic between Chicago and South Shore points that was made possible by the

After a trial with a virtually identical Inland Empire system Baldwin-Westinghouse box cab alternating current locomotive, the Chicago, Lake Shore & South Bend bought two of these 72-ton units for its newly established carload freight business in 1916.—MWEH COLLECTION

From the mid-1920's until the advent of the General Electric "Little Joes" in 1949, heavy Baldwin-Westinghouse steeple cab locomotives dominated the South Shore freight power roster. In the scene at the left, two Baldwin-Westinghouse steeple cabs power a westbound freight through New Carlisle, Indiana.—MWEH COLLECTION (BELOW) A Baldwin Locomotive Works builders photograph of one of the four 80-ton steeple cab units acquired in 1926 under the railroad's first order for new motive power. The illustration was made before installation of electical equipment or final painting.—H. L. BROAD-BELT COLLECTION

friendly Illinois Central connection.

As early as 1918 the South Shore sought to obtain the desired connections through legal means, and was successful in obtaining an order from the Public Service Commission of Indiana compelling the New York Central, the Monon, and several other roads to enter into agreements for connections and interchange. The steam roads appealed the order through the courts, and the case eventually was fought all the way to the U. S. Supreme Court, which finally rendered a decision favorable to the South Shore in 1926.

One of the principal considerations that led to the Insull acquisition of the South Shore was the potential for development of the railroad's freight traffic into a business of major importance. The railway already had the capability to handle the traffic; the Insull utilities empire had the traffic leverage that could help to get it.

The development of South Shore's freight business was among the major objectives of the initial rehabilitation program that began almost immediately after the Insull management took charge in the summer of 1925. Freight stations at principal points were improved and enlarged to handle a greater traffic, and three new freight receiving stations were opened at key locations in Chicago. Through freight rates were established to points in northern Indiana and southern Michigan via the connecting interurban systems of the

These two 53-ton Baldwin-Westinghouse engines were added to the South Shore roster in 1927. Considerably lighter than the railroad's other motive power, they were used in switching service.—CHICAGO SOUTH SHORE & SOUTH BEND

Northern Indiana Railway and the Southern Michigan Railway. The South Shore's initial order for new equipment included four big 80-ton Baldwin-Westinghouse steeple cab locomotives, each of which had an hourly rating of 1,600 h.p. and was capable of a maximum tractive effort of 29,200 pounds.

Even more was going on behind the scenes. Some years before an Insull associate, Colonel Ralph H. James, had been appointed to head a new traffic bureau, whose purpose was to survey and regularize the routing and handling of the Insull group's vast traffic in coal and supplies. Under James, the Insull traffic bureau had long since developed the technique of mobilizing this tremendous traffic to persuade the railroads to cooperate with the Insull companies. Thus, the interchanges that had long been denied the Chicago, Lake Shore & South Bend were soon made available to the new South Shore. Within only a few years the railroad had established interchanges with a total of 13 of the principal connecting steam railroads in its territory. Few railroads were more rigid in their opposition to doing business with electric lines than the New York Central, and as Samuel Insull, Jr. later recalled, "In the case of the South Shore our biggest single difficulty, and final triumph, was to induce the New York Central to connect with the South Shore at South Bend, publish joint rates and divisions, and, finally, to short haul itself, so to speak."

As a matter of course, Insull utilities companies such as the Northern Indiana Public Service Company routed their traffic over the South Shore whenever possible. Of almost equal importance in building South Shore freight traffic was the power of the Insull empire, through a vast network of suppliers and other corporate friends, to influence the routing of traffic over the railroad. Samuel Insull, Jr. illustrates the latter with the example of a sudden bonanza of some 50 cars of coal a day that began being routed over the South Shore via Michigan City to an East Chicago steel plant during the 1920's. Upon checking into the reason for the traffic, Insull found that the traffic manager of an Insull supplier, owed a favor by the steel plant's traffic manager, had asked him, "Can't you ship a little something over the South Shore Line?"

The same sort of imagination and enterprise that went into other aspects of the Insull rehabilitation was also applied to steadily develop the freight business. By 1927 the South Shore had a total of seven LCL freight receiving stations, operated jointly with the North Shore Line and the Chicago, Aurora & Elgin, in the principal shipping districts of Chicago. Tractor trailers delivered freight directly to the South Shore. By means of an arrangement with the Southwestern Michigan Freight Line, a trucking firm, the South Shore established an overnight freight service between Chicago and the Kalamazoo, Michigan, area. Freight was transferred from South Shore trains to trucks at South Bend.

Teamed with one of South Shore's three General Electric steeple cab locomotives, Baldwin-Westinghouse unit No. 1007 led a westbound extra at Bendix siding, just west of South Bend.—MWEH COLLECTION

In 1927, only a year after the Insull-operated North Shore Line inaugurated the first modern "piggyback" trailer-on-flat-car service on any U. S. railroad, the South Shore ordered similar trailers and specially equipped flat cars for its own "ferry truck" service. Operating in overnight trains, the ferry truck service permitted South Shore to offer afternoon pick-up and following morning delivery of trailers between points in the Chicago and South Bend areas.

An expanded traffic department energetically solicited new freight business. Freight traffic advertising was placed regularly in *Traffic World* and other trade publications, stressing the industrial advantages of South Shore Line cities, available industrial sites, convenient interchange points, and the railway's fast carload freight service. The South Shore actively aided new industries to locate along its line. In 1928 the railroad, jointly with several other Midland Utilities subsidiaries, established a $200,000 industrial development loan fund to aid industries to locate in their territory. Within only a few years 15 new industries had located along the South Shore.

The rate of growth for the South Shore's freight traffic after the 1925 Insull takeover was even more spectacular than that for passenger traffic. By 1927 annual freight revenues had almost doubled the 1925 level, and by 1928 had reached almost a million and a quarter dollars — some 550 percent over those for 1925.

The South Shore Line was second only to the Insull-managed North Shore Line in the establishment of a modern "piggyback" service for truck trailers. Special "ferry truck" flat cars transported trailers in an overnight service between Chicago and South Bend from 1927 until the early 1930's. Except for the smaller size of the trailers and the flat car's arch bar trucks, the South Shore's early piggyback equipment was remarkably similar to modern practice today on North American railroads. — C. E. HEDSTROM COLLECTION (**BELOW**) This loaded "ferry truck" flat car was photographed at the Olive Street trailer pit at South Bend in 1934.—MWEH COLLECTION

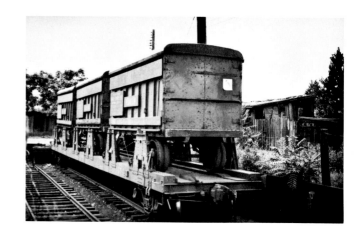

The initial expansion of South Shore freight facilities and equipment soon proved inadequate for the tremendous growth in the traffic. Two 53-ton Baldwin-Westinghouse locomotives were added to the roster for switching service during 1927, and another four 80-ton locomotives, identical to the previous order, were purchased in 1928. Early in 1928 a large new freight station was completed at La Salle Avenue in South Bend, and later the same year another new freight station was completed at Hegewisch, Illinois. Sidings were lengthened and interchange tracks expanded throughout the length of the line. Improvements to passing sidings, track, roadbed, and signalling systems aided the South Shore to improve the quality of its freight service as well as passenger operation.

Freight traffic continued to increase. In 1924 the previous company had handled less than 3,900 loaded freight cars; by 1930 the South Shore was handling over 59,000 loaded cars a year, and annual freight revenues were at a level of well over a million and a half dollars.

Still more motive power was ordered. Three 85-ton steeple cab locomotives were received

Three of these "triple threat" 85-ton General Electric locomotives received in 1930 were designed and equipped for operation on any one of the three Chicago-area Insull interurbans, but spent their entire service life on South Shore.—BOTH GENERAL ELECTRIC COMPANY

Last of the South Shore steeple cabs to survive active service were the three 1930 General Electric 85-tonners. Units No. 1012 and No. 1013 headed a work train at Burns Harbor, Indiana, in 1964. —WILLIAM D. MIDDLETON At the left, 80-ton Baldwin-Westinghouse units No. 1002 and No. 1008 headed a westbound freight at Power siding in Michigan City during 1937.—MWEH COLLECTION (LOWER LEFT) Before their conversion to South Shore orange in 1941 the Illinois Central's big steeple cab locomotives looked like this.—ILLINOIS CENTRAL RAILROAD

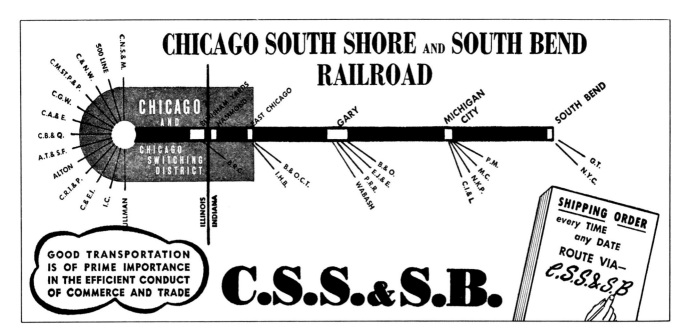

from the General Electric Company in 1930. Designed for operation from either 1,500 or 600 volt direct current, and equipped for pantograph, trolley, or third rail current collection, the locomotives were intended for seasonal use on the two other Chicago-area Insull properties as well as South Shore. Still another 80-ton Baldwin-Westinghouse locomotive was received early the following year, giving South Shore a total of 14 modern freight locomotives.

At South Bend the railroad completed a new $350,000 freight terminal early in 1931. Constructed on a 16-acre tract a mile west of the South Bend business center, the new terminal eliminated the need for freight train movements in city streets, and opened up a new area to industrial development.

After the record year of 1930, freight traffic fell off rapidly in the advancing Depression, and by 1933 annual freight revenues were down to little more than $800,000. Following the collapse of the Insull empire in 1932 the South Shore was on its own once again; no longer did it have behind it the immense power of the Insull companies to control the movement of freight traffic.

But even if the railroad no longer had available the traffic leverage of the Insull group, there remained as an enduring legacy of the Insull era the established interchanges, through rates, and divisions with the South Shore's steam railroad connections which, once

The advertising blotter was one of many aids used by the South Shore to inform the carload shipper of their service. — DONALD DUKE COLLECTION

established, were not easily removed. Realizing that they could no longer count on Insull-controlled freight business, the South Shore set out to utilize these established interchanges and rates to build a more diversified traffic. Freight solicitation efforts were greatly expanded, and within a few years the South Shore had established off-line freight agents in major traffic centers in both the East and West, as well as in the Midwest.

After the low of 1933, freight traffic gradually increased again. By 1941 the steady growth in freight tonnage had presented the South Shore with the problem of a motive power shortage. In 1941 four used 97-ton Baldwin-Westinghouse steeple cab electric locomotives were purchased from the Illinois Central, where they had been rendered surplus by dieselization of Chicago terminal freight switching operations. Constructed in 1929, the four locomotives represented the heaviest units of the steeple cab type ever built by Baldwin-Westinghouse, and each unit was capable of handling a train of 2,500 tons over the South Shore. At the same time, the South Shore sold

Four former Illinois Central Baldwin-Westinghouse units provided South Shore with the motive power muscle to move its unprecedented World War II freight tonnage. No. 901 powers a long eastbound freight through the Indiana countryside at Hicks, a few miles west of Hudson Lake. (LEFT) In this scene, No. 903 is the lead unit in a pair of the 97-ton units heading a westbound freight down 11th Street opposite the South Shore's Michigan City station.—BOTH MWEH COLLECTION

its two light 53-ton freight switchers to New York's Niagara Junction Railway. Even though South Shore's wartime freight ton-miles reached levels as high as 50 percent above that of 1940, the additional motive power represented by the heavy IC units, together with a substantial increase in locomotive miles, was sufficient to get the railroad through the war.

By the end of World War II there could no longer be any doubt that the South Shore had firmly established itself as a major freight carrier. By 1946 the railroad was handling over 83,000 carloads of freight a year and had been earning freight revenues in excess of two million dollars annually ever since 1942. Freight tonnage continued to increase steadily in the years following the war, and from 1950 onward the South Shore's annual freight traffic regularly ran to better than 100,000 loaded cars and its freight revenues from three to four million dollars annually.

In addition to merely increasing the volume of South Shore freight traffic, the railroad's expanded emphasis on freight traffic solicitation had substantially altered the character of the traffic as well. In 1934, for example, coal traffic accounted for some 72 percent of the South Shore's freight business. While successfully retaining this volume of coal traffic, the South Shore was able to develop a much greater volume of diversified agricultural and merchandise traffic, until by the 1950's coal represented only some 35 percent of the railroad's total freight traffic. Exploiting its strategic location interconnecting some 14 trunk lines in the heavily industrialized northwestern Indiana area, and its ability to provide a superior quality of service, the South Shore had successfully attracted an increasing volume of overhead or "bridge" traffic originating and terminating on other lines, which had reached a level of some 70 percent of the railroad's total freight traffic after the end of World War II.

As freight traffic increased steadily during the post-war period, the railroad's fleet of heavy steeple cab locomotives became increasingly inadequate to the task of getting the South Shore's freight tonnage over the road. Consequently, during a period of little more than a

A light snow powdered the ground as a single General Electric steeple cab locomotive headed a six-car eastbound freight eastward through Smith, Indiana, toward South Bend—MWEH COLLECTION

A fleet of big Baldwin-Westinghouse motors constituted the bulwark of South Shore's freight motive power roster from the mid-1920's until "Little Joes" arrived on the property in 1949. Here, two Baldwin-Westinghouse units head a heavy westbound freight across Broadway in Gary, Indiana, in the spring of 1938.—MWEH COLLECTION

Locomotive No. 802 on the left, is shown shortly after its conversion for operation on the South Shore Line by the railroad's Michigan City shops. Clearly visible in this photograph are the mountings for European style buffers blanked off by South Shore in the rebuilding process. — COURTESY OF TRAINS MAGAZINE (RIGHT) The instrument panel and controls of one of the big 2-D-D-2 locomotives, as originally built for delivery to Russia is shown in this builder's photograph taken on General Electric's Erie, Pennsylvania, test track.—GENERAL ELECTRIC COMPANY

decade following the war, the South Shore's roster of freight motive power was almost entirely upgraded from relatively light equipment typical of interurban lines to heavy motive power units characteristic of main line electrification.

The first step in the South Shore's motive power transformation came in 1949, when an unusual circumstance of the post-war international scene provided the railroad with an advantageous means of easing its growing motive power shortage.

In 1946 the Soviet Union had placed an order with the General Electric Company for what were then 20 of the largest electric locomotives ever built. In late 1948, even before the order was completed, the U. S. State Department banned strategic shipments to the U.S.S.R. and the sale was cancelled. GE completed construction of the 20 locomotives and offered them for sale at bargain prices. The South Shore, then actively seeking additional freight power, purchased three of the Russian

units early in 1949. The railroad's resourceful Michigan City shop force undertook the considerable task of rewiring and otherwise modifying the units for operation on South Shore's 1,500 volt D.C. system, and the locomotives entered service late in the year.

Weighing 273 tons in working order, the double-ended 2-D+D-2 units were 88 feet 10 inches long. Eight GE-750 traction motors provided each locomotive with a continuous rating of 5,120 h.p., and a one-hour rating of 5,520 h.p. Continuous tractive effort was 77,000 pounds, with an hourly rating of 85,500 pounds. The maximum permissable speed for the locomotives was 68 m.p.h. Regenerative braking and multiple unit control features originally provided were considered unnecessary for South Shore operations, and were eliminated in the conversion.

The great speed and power of the three locomotives were ideal for the type of fast freight service in which the South Shore specialized, and the "Little Joe" or "Molotov" units, as they

Although all three of the "Little Joe" units acquired by South Shore were completed by the General Electric Company as standard gauge locomotives, they were wired for current collection from 3,300 volt catenary, and the South Shore was obliged to rewire them for 1,500 volt service as well as to remove multiple unit control and regenerative braking features. (ABOVE) Since 1949 the South Shore's three massive 273-ton "Little Joe" locomotives — the equal of electric motive power on the heaviest railroad electrification — have dominated the freight roster of the one-time interurban. No. 803 heads westbound tonnage near Michigan City in 1964. — WILLIAM D. MIDDLETON (LEFT) The last light of day is fading as two eastbound South Shore freights wait for a meet with an eastbound passenger train in a siding between Gary and Michigan City. — JOHN GRUBER

Westbound from South Bend with a short freight, South Shore's ex-New York Central locomotive No. 705 approaches the Chesapeake & Ohio (Pere Marquette) undercrossing just east of the railroad's Michigan City Shops and yard in 1964. (RIGHT) Traction motors and gears grinding, South Shore locomotives No. 701 and No. 703 team up in multiple unit to move the tonnage of a westbound extra out of the yard at Michigan City in the summer of 1963.—BOTH WILLIAM D. MIDDLETON

The engineer of locomotive No. 703 looks back for signals during switching operations at the Michigan City yard in 1963.—WILLIAM D. MIDDLETON (RIGHT) System-wide VHF radio, installed during the late 1940's, helped the service-conscious South Shore to improve the speed and reliability of its freight service. Assistant signal engineer Robert B. Hendrickson utilized the radio in a South Shore locomotive in this 1952 scene.—WALLACE W. ABBEY COURTESY OF TRAINS MAGAZINE

In the gathering twilight of a May evening in 1968, a pair of rebuilt New York Central electrics headed by No. 705 moves out of Burnham Yard with an eastbound freight.—JOHN GRUBER

became popularly known, proved extremely successful on the South Shore Line.

A second opportunity to update its motive power fleet at reasonable cost was presented to the South Shore during the mid-1950's when transfer of electric power from the dieselized Cleveland Union Terminal electrification rendered a number of the New York Central's R-2 class electrics surplus to the needs of the New York terminal electrification. Ten of the C+C units were purchased by South Shore, and between 1955 and 1958 six were extensively rebuilt and rewired by the Michigan City shops for South Shore service, permitting retirement of almost all of the railroads's aging steeple cab locomotive fleet. A seventh rebuilt unit entered service in 1968.

Built by American Locomotive Company and General Electric in 1931, the 140-ton ex-New York Central units were rated at nearly 3,000 h.p. and developed a tractive effort of 66,600 pounds. Equipped for multiple unit control, they could be paired to provide a locomotive equal in capacity to the big Russian units, and had the added virtue of being able to negotiate a number of sidings where weight or clearance limitations precluded operation of the "Little Joes."

During the 1960's the South Shore's freight traffic continued to show promising, if unspectacular, growth. In 1963 freight revenues passed the $4 million mark for the first time, and generally remained above, or close to, that level through the end of the decade. Industrial development efforts by the South Shore brought steady growth in on-line industries. The most spectacular such development was the completion in 1962 of the Northern Indiana Public Service Company's Bailly generating station west of Michigan City, served exclusively by the South Shore. Initially consuming some 10,000 carloads of coal annually, all of it delivered by South Shore unit trains, the plant eventually promised a traffic level of as much as 40,000 annual carloads. The opening of the Burns Harbor plants of Midwest Steel and Bethlehem Steel during the early 1960's, too, helped the continuing growth of South Shore traffic, and the proposed Burns Harbor deep-water port promised more for the future.

151

The era of C&O control brought some fundamental changes to the South Shore's freight operations. The motive power demands of the unit coal-train traffic that came with the opening of the new steel plants and the Bailly generating station proved difficult to meet with the railroad's now aging fleet of electric motive power and the limited capacity of its electrical substations and distribution system. This was resolved in the late 1960's with the acquisition of a fleet of 11 General Motors Electro-Motive GP7 diesel-electric units on the used-equipment market, which largely supplanted the railroad's electric motive power.

This second-hand motive-power fleet was, in turn, replaced a little over a decade later with the delivery of ten brand-new, yellow-clad 2000 h.p. Electro-Motive GP38-2 units early in 1981. These gave the railroad sufficient capacity to replace both the GP7 fleet and the last two elec-

tric motors still in service. The last run for the South Shore's electric freight locomotives came on January 31, 1981, when "Little Joe" unit 803 completed work on a Gary switch run. One of the three big 800 class GE electrics went to scrap, but the other two have been preserved in museums, one at the B&O Museum in Baltimore and the other at the Illinois Railway Museum at Union, Illinois. All were off the property before the end of 1981.

If the South Shore's electric motive power era was over, the new Venango River Corporation owners who took control of the railroad in 1984 decided to recall it with a new traction orange-and-maroon livery for the diesel fleet, patterned after that of the celebrated 800 class electric units. The first two units appeared in the new colors in April 1985, and the remainder followed over the next several years.

(FACING PAGE) In the South Shore's new era of diesel-electric freight operation, a pair of GP38-2 units headed a westbound train at Sheridan, on the west side of Michigan City, in June 1986. Just behind the second unit was one of the special cars for transporting coils of sheet steel; these cars are common on rail lines serving the steel industry at the south end of Lake Michigan. —WILLIAM D. MIDDLETON

Among the legacies of the South Shore's period of Venango River Corporation ownership was a strengthened interchange relationship with Norfolk Southern via a Michigan City connection. The fruits of that connection were evident on June 3, 1995, when SouthShore Extra 2009 took over a unit train of Virginia metallurgical coal destined for Bethlehem Steel's Burns Harbor plant. Three GP38-2 units picked up the 86-car train at the NS interchange adjacent to the electric line's Michigan City shops, and then headed west through the city. Headed by traction orange-and-maroon unit 2009, the massive train temporarily shattered the residential calm as engineer Arnold Niederer cautiously moved his train down Michigan City's 10th Street towards the open track west of town. —NORMAN CARLSON

Free of the constraints of Michigan City traffic, Extra 2009 West headed west through Dune Park at a 35 m.p.h. track speed. Just behind the locomotives is NICTD's handsome new station and headquarters, completed in 1986. The first two GP38-2s boasted the road's newer orange-and-maroon livery reminiscent of the railroad's huge 800-class electric locomotives, while the third unit remained in its original yellow scheme. —NORMAN CARLSON

Its short South Shore journey nearly complete, Extra 2009 west was in the clear for an eastbound passenger train at Bailly. Shortly, the train would head up the Bethlehem Steel lead to the left to complete its journey. —NORMAN CARLSON

6

MICHIGAN CITY

MICHIGAN CITY, Indiana, midway between South Bend and the railroad's junction with the Illinois Central at Kensington, has been headquarters for the South Shore ever since the predecessor Chicago, Lake Shore & South Bend began operation in 1908. Located on the east side of Michigan City, South Shore's headquarters installations include its corporate and operating offices, maintenance shops, and yard facilities that represent the railroad's principal freight operating center.

Original construction plans for the CLS&SB included general office and repair shop facilities at Michigan City which still serve the railroad today. A handsome tile-roofed, white brick building provided space for the South Shore's general office staff, superintendent, and train dispatchers. A large steel truss-roofed, brick shop building, 120 feet wide and 200 feet long, immediately adjacent to the general offices provided space for the three car repair tracks and two tracks for car washing and painting. Repair facilities included two inspection pits, a transfer table, cranes, a 400-ton wheel press, a wheel-turning lathe, and a variety of electrically-powered tools.

Among the major improvements of the Insull era was the construction of a new shop at Michigan City for heavy rolling stock maintenance and overhaul. Constructed of brick, concrete, and steel, and provided with wood block floors, the 32,000 square foot structure represented one of the finest shop installations ever built for an interurban railway. A heavy transfer table afforded access to any of seven repair tracks, three of which were provided with work pits. Repair facilities included completely equipped

In a scene of traditional traction shop activity two members of the Michigan City shop crew roll a repaired Baldwin motor truck back into place on coach No. 26.— WILLIAM D. MIDDLETON

machine, blacksmith, carpenter, wheel and electrical shops. Upon completion of the new structure early in 1931, the original shop building was altered to serve for car inspection and running repairs, and as a paint shop.

In addition to their routine equipment maintenance and repair tasks, the South Shore's skilled and resourceful shop forces have, on occasion, undertaken projects of unusual complexity. During and following World War II the shops carried out the railroad's ambitious program for the lengthening, modernization, and air conditioning of passenger equipment. In 1949 the shops undertook the extensive rewiring and modification work required to adapt three of the famous 273-ton General Electric "Little Joe" locomotives for the South Shore operation. More recently, seven former New York Central R-2 class electric locomotives were extensively rewired and rebuilt for service on South Shore.

On the opposite page, a pair of 700-class ex-New York Central freight locomotives running light through the Michigan City yard. The two engines have just brought in a freight train and are moving toward the shops for an inspection before making another run.— ROBERT HEGGE

Standing between the venerable shop and headquarters building that saw the passage of the old Chicago, Lake Shore & South Bend Railway's first train, combine No. 110 headed South Bend-Chicago train No. 28 in the summer of 1963. In the siding alongside a pair of 700-class freight locomotives waited to follow the passenger run with a westbound freight.—WILLIAM D. MIDDLETON

In the two scenes above, two members of the Michigan City shop crew go about the task of replacing a traction motor in one of South Shore's big Baldwin trucks. Since new trucks are no longer available, the South Shore keeps all motors and trucks in fine operating condition.—BOTH WILLIAM D. MIDDLETON (LEFT)
Few railroad shops of comparable size have attempted work any more ambitious than South Shore's program for lengthening and modernizing its heavy steel passenger cars. In the view at the left, coach No. 23 has been cut in two for lengthening in 1947. In the lower view, combine No. 101 is receiving its large "picture" windows and air conditioning equipment in 1949. — BOTH MWEH COLLECTION

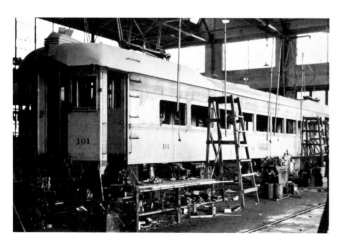

A more recent program undertaken by the Michigan City shops has been the extensive rebuilding and modification work carried out from 1955 onward to convert former New York Central R-2 class locomotives to South Shore's 700 class, seven of which have entered service. In the view above, five of the New York Central units await conversion at the shops in 1956.—STEPHEN D. MAGUIRE (RIGHT) In July 1955, ex-New York Central No. 314 was well along on its conversion to South Shore No. 702.— WILLIAM D. MIDDLETON

Looking as good as new, South Shore "Little Joe" No. 803 glistens in a fresh coat of paint at the Michigan City paint shop in 1963.—R. OLMSTED (RIGHT) Fresh from the Michigan City rebuild bay in the summer of 1955, the first of the rebuilt New York Central units — No. 701 — was photographed alongside No. 1004, one of the first South Shore Baldwin-Westinghouse steeple cabs delivered in 1926.—WILLIAM D. MIDDLETON

Operating from the South Shore's Michigan City headquarters building, a single dispatcher controls the entire railroad. The day trick DS made an entry on his train sheet in 1964.—WILLIAM D. MIDDLETON

Car 1 has been raised on jacks and the trucks removed to begin overhaul. In the background, work continues on car 17. —WILLIAM D. MIDDLETON

In 1997, NICTD completed a major new engineering building and overhaul shop at Michigan City and began a "mid-life" overhaul program for the Nippon Sharyo car fleet acquired in the early 1980's. In April 1998, one of the first of the fleet to begin the program was car 1, which had just been raised on jacks to remove its trucks. —WILLIAM D. MIDDLETON

7

THE ROAD TO NICTD

The primary reason for the South Shore's affiliation with a larger carrier in the 1960's had been to strengthen its competitive position for freight traffic in the face of continuing mergers in the East, and to assure a supply of cars that would permit the line to serve effectively the new Bethlehem Steel plant at Burns Harbor. This had been achieved when the C&O took control of the railroad early in 1967, and the South Shore's freight business prospered. By the early 1970's South Shore freight earnings ranged from more than $8 million to nearly $10 million annually, accounting for close to 70 percent of total operating revenues.

Despite freight profits, however, the line proved anything but the money maker that the C&O had anticipated, as losses from the passenger business continued to mount. By the beginning of the 1970's, the passenger deficit was running as high as $2 million annually, more than enough in most years to offset net earnings from freight. By mid-1970 the railroad was talking about the likelihood of ending all passenger ser-

vice, but had to settle instead for a major reduction in service that was authorized by the Interstate Commerce Commission in May 1972.

By 1976 the South Shore was at a crisis point. The annual passenger deficit had hit a record level of $2.6 million in 1975, the accumulated 1966–75 deficit totaled more than $14.5 million, and not once during that ten-year period had the South Shore paid a dividend to its stockholders.

Adding urgency to the situation was the condition of the South Shore's 50-year-old passenger-car fleet. Replacement parts and components for the obsolete cars had become increasingly difficult to obtain; many had to be fabricated in the South Shore's own shops. Maintenance costs had risen to extremely high levels, while the availability of equipment had deteriorated. A structural evaluation by consulting engineers Louis T. Klauder and Associates in 1976 concluded that the equipment was worn out and should be removed from service as soon as possible.

As far back as the late 1960's the South Shore

Headed by car 1, the first of a third generation of South Shore passenger cars, two-car eastbound train 303 (a Sunday-only Chicago–South Bend schedule) approached the Emery Road undercrossing at Hudson Lake, Indiana, on a warm July morning in 1983. —WILLIAM D. MIDDLETON

had begun an effort to seek some form of public support for its passenger operations under the provisions of the federal Urban Mass Transportation Assistance Act of 1964. But a combination of Indiana fiscal conservatism and the political complications of the line's two-state, five-county service territory repeatedly frustrated efforts to form a local agency through which public funds could be channeled to support the South Shore's passenger services.

Some help had begun to come from Illinois in 1973, when the state's Department of Transportation provided a $230,705 grant to help offset the South Shore's passenger losses within Illinois. This support continued through the newly formed Regional Transportation Authority (RTA) the following year, but it met only a small part of the need to offset a loss on passenger service that was now approaching $2 million annually.

By early 1976, with no visible progress toward forming an Indiana public agency to support the service, the C&O-controlled South Shore was ready to discontinue passenger service. In March the railroad announced that it would put a million dollars into interim equipment repairs to buy time for a public agency to come up with a new-car program. If such a program had not materialized within six months, said South Shore president Albert W. Dudley, the railroad "will have no choice but to pursue a course of action leading to cessation of all passenger operations."

To long-time observers of efforts to establish a public-transportation agency in northwestern Indiana, the result was probably predictable. Despite efforts at both the local and state levels to find a solution, nothing happened, and the South Shore set out to do just what it said it would. Before the end of 1976 the railroad had filed a petition with the Interstate Commerce Commission to end all passenger operations.

In April 1977 the ICC told the South Shore to

The remarkable heavy steel cars of the South Shore's Insull era of the late 1920's endured in demanding, high-speed passenger service well into their sixth decade. Each of them rolled up something on the order of three million miles of service. The last years of the old order were at hand on July 21, 1979, when car 25 raced eastward at Fail Road, near Smith in La Porte County, Indiana, running as train 463—a Saturday, Sunday and holiday Chicago–South Bend schedule. Built by Pullman in 1927, the car had been lengthened and modernized shortly after World War II. — WILLIAM D. MIDDLETON

continue running its passenger trains for another ten months. "We expect this will be sufficient time for the State of Indiana to take steps to save the service," said the ICC order. "If this does not occur, we think it likely that there is no future for the South Shore's passenger operations." The ruling, in effect, gave government ten months to come to grips with the problem, after which it seemed quite clear that the Commission would allow the South Shore to shut down passenger service if no solution had been found.

This, finally, did the trick.

That same month the Indiana General Assembly passed legislation introduced earlier in the year that enabled the four Indiana counties through which the South Shore operated, Lake, Porter, LaPorte, and St. Joseph, to form the Northern Indiana Commuter Transportation District (NICTD), an agency through which federal, state, and local funds could be made available to support South Shore passenger service. Unfortunately, the legislation did not give NICTD any taxing authority, a shortcoming that has handicapped the agency's efforts to rebuild the railroad ever since.

Beginning in 1978, the limited support of passenger operating costs coming through the Chicago area RTA was supplemented by federal operating-assistance funds and grants through NICTD from Indiana's Public Mass Transportation Fund and, in 1981, from the Commuter Rail Service Fund, which was funded from a state tax on leased rail cars. It would not be until 1982 that public funding would fully offset the South Shore's passenger deficit, but the additional support helped to keep the service going.

Even more important to the long-term future of South Shore passenger operations was NICTD's capital-improvement program, which would at last bring a new fleet of passenger cars to the railroad. The foundation for this program was a 1978 cost-benefit study of the South Shore corridor completed by Indiana University's Institute for Urban Transportation. This study had found that retention of South Shore service was the least costly and most beneficial option for the region, and had recommended a program of capital improvements for the railroad's passenger service.

During 1979 NICTD developed a $67.5-million capital program that would be funded from an 80 percent federal share and a variety of state and local fund sources. Its principal component was an entirely new third generation of modern cars for South Shore passenger service. Bids were taken early in 1979 and a contract awarded the following year to the Sumitomo Corporation of America for 36 cars, later increased to a total of 44 cars, at a total cost of $47 million. Built by Japan's Nippon Sharyo, these were 85-foot, air-conditioned, stainless-steel cars comparable to main-line electric multiple-unit equipment. Each car could seat 93 passengers and was arranged with end doors and traps for high- or low-level platform loading, and a wide center door on each side for high-level platforms. All 44 were motor cars, each powered by four General Electric motors with an hourly rating of 160 h.p. and capable of driving the 57.5-ton cars at a 75 m.p.h. balancing speed.

Car bodies and trucks were manufactured in Japan, while traction motors, control systems, braking systems, air conditioning, seating, and other components were made in the U.S. Final assembly of the cars was completed at a General Electric plant in Cleveland.

But delivery of these new cars was still several years away, and the five-year period between the formation of NICTD and the replacement of the South Shore passenger-car fleet would prove a troubled one for the railroad and its passengers. To bridge the gap until the new cars could enter service, the South Shore had continued a program of structural reinforcement for the old cars recommended by the 1976 Klauder study, and had made a number of improvements to electrical and braking systems to improve their resistance to severe winter-weather conditions. Even so, the aging car fleet grew increasingly unreliable, and the South Shore experienced some extraordinary service problems.

The South Shore's performance hit what was probably its nadir in the winter of 1977–78, when the railroad was confronted with one of its worst winters in decades. In January, under the combined effects of extreme cold weather and a fine, blowing snow, traction motors, field coils, motor-generator sets, and other components began to fail at an alarming rate. Equipment availability quickly fell below the 34-car minimum required

The winter of 1977–78 was the worst to hit the South Shore in decades. In a heavy blizzard on the morning of January 14, 1978, westbound Michigan City–Chicago train 366 approached the beginning of street running in Michigan City's 11th Street. With most of its equipment disabled by the bitter weather, the railroad soon shut down all passenger service. —DONALD R. KAPLAN

When severe winter weather again disabled much of the South Shore's aging passenger car fleet in January 1982, the railroad managed to maintain service only by leasing two RTA diesel-hauled push-pull train sets. Running in push mode as westbound train 62, one of them pounded through crossings with the Louisville & Nashville and Conrail on the west side of Michigan City on a snowy March 26, 1982. —DONALD R. KAPLAN

to maintain a full level of service. On January 13th, with only a dozen operable cars left, South Shore president Dudley made the decision to shut the railroad down. It was another week before any passenger service was restored, and it was not until the end of April that the railroad was again operating its full schedule of service.

There was more trouble to come before the new cars were on the scene.

The winter of 1981–82 was another hard one. In some of the most bitterly cold weather ever recorded in northwestern Indiana, there were numerous wire breaks in the South Shore catenary. At some of the shorter breaks, motormen simply dropped their pantographs and coasted under the wire break, while at other, longer breaks shuttle-bus services were established to carry passengers around the gaps. The extreme cold and heavy snows again brought electrical problems for the line's aging cars. The number of available cars dropped as low as 17 as the Michigan City shop crews struggled to repair burned-out traction motors and other electrical components. By January 25 the South Shore had adopted an emergency schedule based upon the use of two diesel-powered push-pull train sets leased from the RTA and what South Shore cars remained operable.

Even as the South Shore struggled to maintain any service at all, an initial prototype car for the new fleet arrived at Michigan City to begin test operation early in 1982. The first five production cars arrived in Michigan City in August to begin acceptance testing. New cars began operating in regular service in November 1982. Following acceptance of the last eight add-on cars, the South Shore ended operation of the last of its 1920's Insull-era cars the following September. By this time well past the 50-year mark, each of these enduring steel cars had accumulated something on the order of three million miles of service. As they rolled into retirement they took with them a record of longevity in the most demanding sort of high-speed passenger service—a record that had seldom been equaled anywhere in interurban railroading.

In addition to the purchase of new cars, NICTD's capital improvement program for the South Shore included major improvements to the railroad's power supply and equipment maintenance capacity. To provide needed additional power capacity, the RTA installed new electrical substations at Monroe Street in downtown Chicago and at Hegewisch, while new equipment was installed at all nine of the railroad's existing substations between Hammond and South Bend.

By September 25, 1983, the South Shore's old steel cars had gone out in style. The Northern Indiana Commuter Transportation District issued this ticket for commemorative trips on the last day. —NORTHERN INDIANA COMMUTER TRANSPORTATION DISTRICT

The start-up of revenue service with the new equipment was marked by "dedication day" ceremonies at Michigan City on October 23, 1982. NICTD issued this commemorative ticket for the occasion. —NORTHERN INDIANA COMMUTER TRANSPORTATION DISTRICT

The big 85-foot Nippon Sharyo cars that began to enter South Shore service in 1982 were comparable in every way to the best electric multiple-unit equipment operating anywhere in North America. The gleaming stainless-steel cars looked their best under the lights of the South Bend station on a July evening in 1983. The two-car train had just arrived from Chicago as eastbound train 25. —WILLIAM D. MIDDLETON

Additional feeder cable was installed to better balance the power supply. Shop improvements to support the new equipment at Michigan City included new overhead traveling cranes, a drop table for truck changeouts, a wheel truing machine, lengthening of shop tracks and inspection pits, expanding the shop building, a car washer, and improvements to the building itself.

Despite all of the equipment problems or winter weather disruptions, South Shore passenger traffic began to grow again even before the new equipment was on hand. From a record low of less than 1.5 million passengers in 1978, ridership grew by a modest 100,000 in 1979, and then jumped by over half a million, to 2.1 million, in 1980. By 1983, as the railroad completed its transition to the new passenger fleet, traffic was back up to 2.5 million annual riders, its highest level since 1970.

With the critical capital improvements needed for a restored South Shore passenger service now complete, NICTD turned its attention to its relationship with the railroad. A tri-party, five-year agreement reached late in 1981 by NICTD, the Chicago area RTA, and the South Shore had given the two public agencies the authority to set fares, determine train schedules, and approve the railroad's budgets, but it had also obligated them to fully fund the South Shore's passenger losses as well as a "reasonable return on investment." Still without any authority to levy any taxes for local funding shares, and with the new Reagan administration in Washington proposing cuts in federal operating assistance to transit, NICTD began to look for other ways of assuring the future of South Shore passenger service.

Outright ownership of the railroad looked like an attractive option, since it offered the possibility of substantially offsetting the passenger-service deficit with profits from freight operation. While the annual passenger deficit was then running at a little over $4 million annually, the South Shore's before-tax freight service profits had been ranging anywhere from $4 million to $7 million annually. Early in 1984 the Indiana General Assembly passed enabling legislation that would permit NICTD to acquire ownership of the South Shore.

NICTD's hopes to acquire the South Shore, however, were dashed in September 1984 when the C&O sold the railroad for $31.7 million to the Venango River Corporation, a group of five Illinois and Indiana businessmen, all but one of them former Santa Fe managers.

NICTD soon signed a purchase-of-service contract with Venango River, and, for a time, the new arrangement looked promising. The new owners aggressively sought to recapture some of the local and overhead freight traffic that the railroad had lost, talked about extending westward to tap new freight connections at Chicago, and planned an expanded trailer-on-flat-car service. Venango planned to develop a passenger excursion market, and talked of its intention to restore hourly service between Chicago and South Bend and half-hourly service between Chicago and Gary. The railroad's GP38-2 diesels began to appear in a traditional South Shore orange-and-maroon color scheme reminiscent of the celebrated 800-class electric locomotives.

Things soon turned sour for the "Venango River boys," however. The root of their misfortune turned out to be an ill-advised move to expand the Venango railroad empire. In May 1987 Venango paid $81 million to acquire 631 miles of line from Illinois Central Gulf that essentially represented the former Chicago & Alton, extending from Joliet, Illinois, to St. Louis, and from Springfield, Illinois, to Kansas City. Although the new acquisition would be

Hudson Lake, west of South Bend, once a popular destination for summer outings via the South Shore Line, remains an attractive feature of the northern Indiana landscape along the electric line. A two-car train of new cars, westbound as South Bend–Chicago train 10, sped past the lake in July 1983. —WILLIAM D. MIDDLETON

Operation through the residential streets of Michigan City, Indiana, remains to this day a reminder of the South Shore's interurban heritage. A two-car train of the big Nippon Sharyo cars seemed incongruous in the extreme as it lumbered down Michigan City's 11th Street in July 1983. The train was eastbound Chicago–Michigan City train 107. —WILLIAM D. MIDDLETON

With the slow drag through the streets of Michigan City behind it, Sunday and holiday-only South Bend–Chicago train 304 had begun to pick up speed as it approached the Highway 12 crossing west of the city in the summer of 1983.
—WILLIAM D. MIDDLETON

operated separately as the Chicago, Missouri & Western, it would have a direct link with the South Shore via ICG trackage rights.

The price paid for the CM&W turned out to be too high, and revenues too low. By April 1988 the line had filed for bankruptcy and was eventually sold off to Southern Pacific and Gateway Western. Things were not going well for Venango's South Shore, either. The line had loaned $4 million to the CM&W before it went bankrupt, and the freight service had not proved as profitable as expected. By the end of 1988 the cash-short South Shore had defaulted on principal and interest payments, and Citicorp, its principal creditor, called in its loan and took over management of the line. Venango put the South Shore up for sale, and then, in April 1989, filed for Chapter 11 bankruptcy protection.

Relations between NICTD and the railroad

had begun to deteriorate soon after Venango took over. The two parties were soon embroiled in a dispute over costs for operating the passenger service, which began to increase rapidly after the new owners took over. Still without an adequate local funding source, NICTD fell behind in meeting its obligation to cover the South Shore's passenger-service losses. As early as the end of 1985, with NICTD some $5.7 million behind in its payments, the railroad was threatening to shut down or drastically reduce passenger service. This was staved off in March 1986 by an emergency loan to NICTD from the State of Indiana, while a study commission wrestled with the problem of a permanent funding source. Little changed until late in 1988. Locked in a dispute with NICTD over claims for payment and liability insurance, the South Shore obtained ICC approval to discontinue all passenger ser-

A modern view of the South Shore's celebrated "Ideal Section" at Miller, Indiana, found it looking better than ever with a train of brand new stainless-steel cars operating over welded-rail track founded in heavy crushed-rock ballast. Car 18 headed a westbound four-car Michigan City–Chicago train 114 on July 15, 1983. —WILLIAM D. MIDDLETON

Westbound from Michigan City to Chicago on July 14, 1983, a two-car train 118 soared over the Baltimore & Ohio overcrossing on the east side of Gary, Indiana. Visible in the foreground is the interchange track used by South Shore freight trains. —WILLIAM D. MIDDLETON

vice at the end of the year, but then deferred the move to mid-1989. The resulting financial crisis brought the railroad to bankruptcy early in 1989.

Venango's bankruptcy, as it turned out, gave NICTD another chance to acquire the South Shore, and a new era began on January 1, 1990. In a complex financial arrangement, the investment-banking firm Anacostia & Pacific Company paid $34.6 million to take over the railroad from a bankrupt Venango, which now became the Chicago SouthShore & South Bend. The deal provided that NICTD would eventually acquire ownership of all of the South Shore's Indiana trackage and facilities that were used for both passenger and freight service, while SouthShore would retain all freight-only trackage and exclusive freight rights on NICTD tracks. Federal and state funds financed the $16.8 million transaction, which was concluded early the following year. In Illinois, where the electric line operated over the Illinois Central–owned Kensington & Eastern between the state line and the junction with Metra Electric's former IC suburban system at 115th Street, an opposite ownership structure emerged. Here, the freight carrier acquired ownership of the K&E from the IC in 1996, while NICTD retained a perpetual lease of the line.

At last, NICTD had its own railroad!

While South Shore ownership was going through these turbulent times, NICTD and other public agencies continued a program of capital improvements for passenger service. In June 1984, the City of Gary, the Indiana Toll Road Commission, and the Federal Highway Administration completed a new Gary Metro Center that gave the South Shore an elevated line through downtown Gary as well as new station facilities shared with local and intercity buses. In June 1986, NICTD completed a new Dune Park station at Chesterton, Indiana, at the intersection of Indiana 49 with U.S. Highway 12. Designed in an architectural style reminiscent of the "Insull Spanish" stations of the 1920's, the new station also included space for an on-line headquarters for the agency. In May 1988 the RTA completed platform improvements to accommodate the new South Shore cars at the

Eastbound Chicago-Gary train 205 entered the bypass around East Chicago, Indiana, on July 15, 1983. The four-car train was running against the flow of morning rush-hour traffic after completing an early trip into Chicago. At Gary, the equipment would change direction again to haul a second load of commuters into the Loop. —WILLIAM D. MIDDLETON

Hegewisch is the South Shore's only passenger station in Illinois before it joins the Metra Electric at 115th Street, and it originates more passengers than any other station on the railroad. Loop-bound commuters boarded westbound Michigan City–Chicago train 108 during the morning rush period on July 15, 1983. The size of the crowd justified plans to build high-level platforms at the station. —WILLIAM D. MIDDLETON

Randolph Street station in Chicago shared with Metra Electric suburban services.

The availability of the new passenger cars and other improvements, together with a new emphasis on marketing and promoting South Shore service, contributed to steady gains in passenger traffic. Football specials for Notre Dame games at South Bend operated again. Special services and fares helped to generate a lively off-peak traffic to special events and attractions in Chicago or along the South Shore's route. By 1988 the line's annual passenger count topped 3 million, its highest level in 20 years, and it was still growing.

This growth in traffic soon outstripped the capacity of the South Shore passenger fleet, and standing passengers became the norm on the most popular rush-hour schedules. More cars were needed, but finding the money to buy them would prove a difficult task for NICTD. A package of state and federal funds was finally put together in 1990, and early the following year NICTD placed a $26.5 million order with Nippon Sharyo for 17 new cars that were generally similar to the ones ordered a decade earlier. Placed in service in late 1992 and early 1993, the order included ten non-motorized trailers and seven motor cars, three of them replacement cars which utilized trucks and other components from wreck-damaged equipment. A major difference from the original equipment was the use of high-density 3-2 seating to provide greater capacity for the railroad's crowded rush-hour trains.

At the same time, state and federal funding became available for still more improvements to South Shore stations and other facilities. One of the most important of these was a new South Bend terminal. Ever since 1970, when the South Shore had cut back its service from the downtown South Bend terminal at La Salle Avenue and Michigan Street, trains had terminated at a shabby concrete-block station at Bendix, on the west side of the city. A lack of secure parking or transit connections, and the station's location in a marginal neighborhood had helped to discourage potential riders.

A new South Bend terminal was created by bringing the trains right into the Michiana Re-

Eastbound train 107 crossed the massive steel-truss bridge that carries the South Shore's double-track line over the Calumet River between 115th Street and Hegewisch. The six-car train was enroute from the Chicago Loop to Michigan City on July 15, 1983. —WILLIAM D. MIDDLETON

gional Airport, utilizing upgraded existing industrial trackage and a mile of new track financed by the airport authority. NICTD built new high-level platforms at the terminal, and the airport provided station facilities in an expanded terminal building. Trains began running to the new terminal in November 1992, and traffic in and out of South Bend soon increased by 50 to 75 percent. By late 1997, service to South Bend had been increased to five round trips on weekdays and nine weekend and holiday round trips, its highest level in 25 years.

Also in 1992, the RTA completed a handsome new station at Hegewisch, one of the South Shore's busiest stations. Parking capacities were increased at other stations. Over a period of several years, the existing 100-pound rail between Michigan City and South Bend was welded to complete conversion of the entire South Shore main line to continuous welded rail.

In 1993 NICTD began the installation of a modern computer-based ticketing system. By the end of 1994 NICTD had completed a new general office building and station at the Michigan City Shops, and work began on expanded parking facilities and a new station with high-level platforms at Hammond. In Gary, construction began on an additional bridge over Conrail and

The South Shore's Mitchell A. Markovitz, every inch the properly attired engineer, takes a radio train order during a run from Chicago to Gary at the controls of eastbound train 209. An accomplished artist and designer, Markovitz also doubles as the railroad's graphic designer. — WILLIAM D. MIDDLETON

Norfolk Southern tracks east of Clark Road to eliminate the gantlet bridge that had been the scene of a major collision early in 1993.

By 1998, with passenger traffic up to almost 3.4 million passengers per year, NICTD adopted a six-year, $88 million capital-improvement program designed to improve reliability, reduce running times to the Chicago Loop, and increase the rush-hour capacity of South Shore service. A new 30,000 square foot building completed at Michigan City provided space for the railroad's engineering and maintenance-of-way organization, as well as room to begin a "mid-life" rehabilitation program for the 1982 car fleet. Acquisition of another eight to ten passenger cars to reduce overcrowding on rush-hour trains was initiated. Alternating current propulsion equipment, which promised both lower maintenance costs and higher performance, was planned for both the new cars and the existing fleet as it went through overhaul.

New passenger shelters and expanded parking were completed at Miller and Ogden Dunes, and

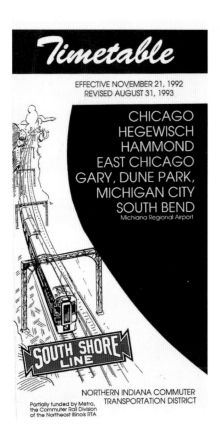

The handsome design of contemporary South Shore timetables and promotional materials recalls the elegant award-winning art work of the railroad's Insull era of the 1920's. —NORTHERN INDIANA COMMUTER TRANSPORTATION DISTRICT

Northern Indiana Commuter Transportation District general manager Gerald R. Hanas has guided the program to preserve and rehabilitate South Shore passenger service ever since the agency's formation in 1977. —NORTHERN INDIANA COMMUTER TRANSPORTATION DISTRICT

the historic "Insull Spanish" station at Beverly Shores was restored. During 1998, engineering was begun for a $9 million new station with high-level platforms and expanded parking at East Chicago, while high-level platforms were planned for the Hegewisch station and the Gary Metro Center. With the completion of this planned high-level platform work at its busiest stations, together with the improved equipment performance that a shift to a.c. propulsion would bring, NICTD was anticipating that it could reduce Michigan City–Chicago running times by as much as 12 to 14 minutes.

Completion of a new bridge over Burns Waterway in 1997 was the key element of a project that by the end of 1999 would link the existing Wilson and Wagner passing sidings to create 6.5 miles of additional double track east of Gary. Eventually, NICTD plans to expand its double track 14.4 miles east from Emerson to Dune Park station. Six aging bridges were scheduled for replacement.

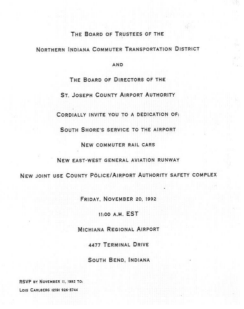

THE BOARD OF TRUSTEES OF THE

NORTHERN INDIANA COMMUTER TRANSPORTATION DISTRICT

AND

THE BOARD OF DIRECTORS OF THE

ST. JOSEPH COUNTY AIRPORT AUTHORITY

CORDIALLY INVITE YOU TO A DEDICATION OF:

SOUTH SHORE'S SERVICE TO THE AIRPORT

NEW COMMUTER RAIL CARS

NEW EAST-WEST GENERAL AVIATION RUNWAY

NEW JOINT USE COUNTY POLICE/AIRPORT AUTHORITY SAFETY COMPLEX

FRIDAY, NOVEMBER 20, 1992

11:00 A.M. EST

MICHIANA REGIONAL AIRPORT

4477 TERMINAL DRIVE

SOUTH BEND, INDIANA

RSVP BY NOVEMBER 11, 1992 TO:
LOIS CARLBERG (219) 926-5744

November 20, 1992, was a big day for both the South Shore and the Michiana Regional Airport at South Bend. NICTD and the St. Joseph County Airport Authority issued this Dedication Day invitation to celebrate the opening of the railroad's new passenger terminal at the airport and the delivery of another 17 new South Shore cars, as well as the opening of new airport facilities. NICTD ran a special train to the celebration from Hegewisch, Illinois. —NORTHERN INDIANA COMMUTER TRANSPORTATION DISTRICT

Brand new Nippon Sharyo car 45 headed the inaugural train that burst through a banner to celebrate the opening of the South Shore's new Michiana Regional Airport station at South Bend. —GARY MILLS PHOTOGRAPHY/NORTHERN INDIANA COMMUTER TRANSPORTATION DISTRICT

Sheltered by a high canopy with a raised skylight, and provided with high-level platforms, the South Shore's new South Bend station is linked directly with the Michiana Regional Airport concourse. —NORTHERN INDIANA COMMUTER TRANSPORTATION DISTRICT

Still other long-range improvements for the South Shore were contemplated: the elimination of grade crossings, and track realignment that could permit higher speeds. Enhanced safety and train control would be provided by a modern communications-based signaling installation with cab signals that would permit 90 m.p.h. operation and a centralized traffic-control system for the entire railroad.

Still in the future is a long-planned line relocation at Michigan City that will replace the South Shore's last section of interurban-style street running through 10th and 11th streets in the city. The most likely of several schemes for this would utilize a combination of South Shore freight track, and Amtrak and Norfolk Southern tracks to reroute South Shore trains to the north through downtown Michigan City. The South Shore and Amtrak would share a new passenger station.

Somewhere in the future, too, could be the first expansion of South Shore service since the railroad was completed in 1907. In 1997 consultants began the first phase of work on a major investment study that is considering the development of rail service in a West Lake Corridor linking western Lake County with Chicago. The projected service would extend south on a 4.5-mile right-of-way (former Monon track, already owned by NICTD and the communities of Munster and Hammond) running from Hammond to Airline Junction. The new service would then run either south to Lowell, Indiana, over a CSX Transportation line; southeast to Crown Point, Indiana, over an abandoned Conrail line; or east over CN to Valparaiso. A long below-grade or elevated-grade separation for existing streets and rail lines would be re-

(FACING PAGE) On April 21, 1998, westbound train 18 for Chicago waited for its 12:01 p.m. departure time from the South Shore's new South Bend station at the Michiana Regional Airport. —WILLIAM D. MIDDLETON

173

As part of a program to shorten running times between Michigan City and Chicago, NICTD in 1997 began the construction of high-level platforms that are expected to reduce station dwell times at its most heavily used stations from Gary to Hegewisch. The first installation completed was at the railroad's new Hammond, Indiana, station, where a novel gantlet track arrangement actuated by a V-tag control system directs freight trains away from the platforms. Eastbound Chicago-Gary train 209 stopped there on April 20, 1998. —WILLIAM D. MIDDLETON

quired to link the new route with the existing South Shore line west of the Hammond station.

The study also considered track changes at the Kensington interlocking (where the South Shore joins Metra Electric) and signaling improvements that could increase capacity and reduce running times over the jointly used Metra Electric line between 115th Street and Randolph Street—already Chicago's busiest commuter corridor.

Without question, the South Shore Line had much to be proud of as it rolled toward its centennial. What at one time might have been voted the interurban "least likely to succeed" had, after all, managed to survive intact while all of the others had failed. Once again rebuilt and transformed, the railroad remained a vital transportation resource to the Chicago South Shore communities it had served for so long. One could, with fair confidence, predict that the trains would continue to roll under northwestern Indiana catenary well into the 21st century.

APPENDIX

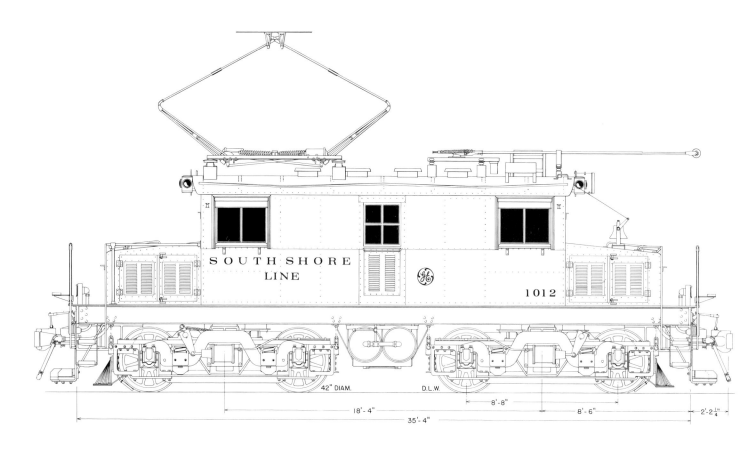

42" DIAM.   D.L.W.   8'-8"   8'-6"   2'-2 1/4"

18'-4"

35'-4"

SCALE—3/16 inch to the foot

Scale Drawing by David L. Waddington

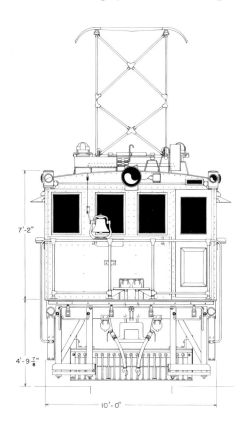

7'-2"

4'-9 7/8"

10'-0"

SOUTH SHORE
LOCOMOTIVES NO. 1011-1013

SPECIFICATIONS
AND DATA

Type—Steeple Cab B-B
Builder—Baldwin-General Electric
Date Built—1929 and 1930
Builders Nos.—No. 1011—11075, No. 1012—
     11076, No. 1013—11339
Length Overall—39 feet 8½ inches
Width Overall—10 feet
Height Overall—12 feet
Total Engine Weight—160,000 pounds
Driving Wheel Diameter—42 inches
Trucks—Baldwin
Motors—Four GE 704A
Control—HBF
Horsepower—1,600 h.p.
Tractive Effort—29,200 pounds

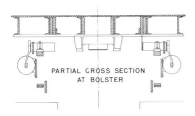

PARTIAL CROSS SECTION
AT BOLSTER

Purchased in 1929, the South Shore's three big 80-ton General Electric steeple cab locomotives outlasted all the railroad's other similar power, and remained in service well into the 1960's. In the view above, No. 1012 is seen in a yard view. (BELOW) Two generations of Erie-built General Electric power wait between assignments in the Michigan City yard. The two 1930-vintage interurban style steeple cabs were dwarfed by two of South Shore's massive 800-class 2-D-D-2 locomotives of 1949.—ROBERT HEGGE

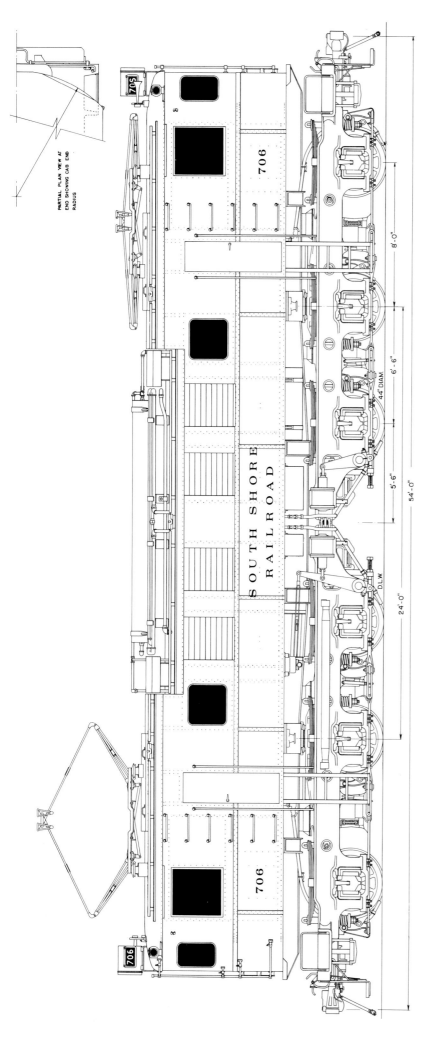

SOUTH SHORE LOCOMOTIVES NO. 701-707

SPECIFICATIONS AND DATA

Length Overall—54 feet
Width Overall—9 feet 10 inches
Height Overall—12 feet 9 inches
Total Engine Weight—280,000 pounds
Driving Wheel Diameter—44 inches
Gear Ratio—3.45—69/20
Brake Equipment—14 EL

Trucks—General Steel Castings
Motors—Six GE 286B
Control—PCL (MU)
Horsepower—3,000 h.p.
Tractive Effort—66,600 pounds at 25% adhesion
70,000 pounds for a 280,000 pound locomotive
Maximum Speed—60 m.p.h.

Type—C-C
Builder—American Locomotive-General Electric
Date Built—1930 and 1931
Builders Nos.

South Shore No.	Alco No.	GE No.
701	68236	11159
702	68242	11165
703	68231	11154
704	68271	11194
705	68268	11191
706	68269	11192
707	68270	11193

NOTE

South Shore Nos. 701-706 were rebuilt during 1955-1958. No. 707 was rebuilt in 1968. The pantographs, compressors, motor blowers, series parallel switches are from former Cleveland Union Terminal 700 class electric locomotives.

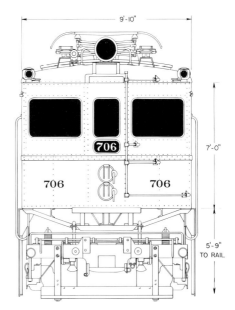

SCALE—3/16 inch to the foot

Scale Drawing by David L. Waddington

The first of South Shore's seven rebuilt New York Central R-2 Class C-C locomotives reveals some interesting variations in the details of the work performed by the railroad's Michigan City shops. In this view, No. 701, the first unit rebuilt in 1955, is shown about to depart from Michigan City with a westbound freight in 1963.—WILLIAM D. MIDDLETON

Locomotive No. 707 is the last of South Shore's rebuilt New York Central R-2 Class engines, and it was completed more than a decade later, in fact 1968. Among the most noticeable changes were sealed headlights and the high-visibility zebra striped front end paint scheme.—JOHN A. MORRIS

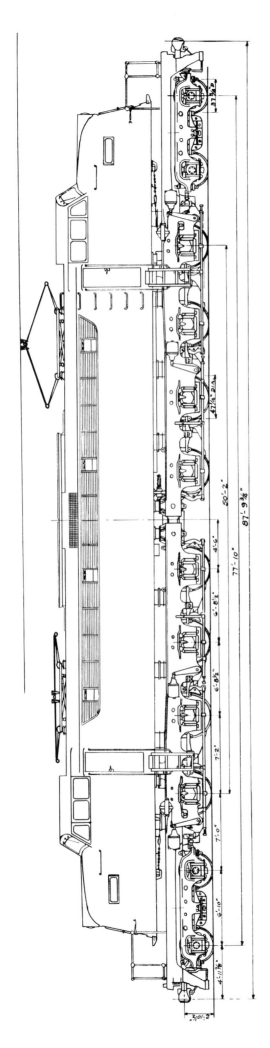

SOUTH SHORE LOCOMOTIVES NO. 801-803

SPECIFICATIONS AND DATA

Type—2-D-D-2
Builder—General Electric
Date Built—May 1949
Builders Nos.

South Shore No.	GE No.	Road No.
801	29930	A2318
802	29931	A2319
803	29932	A2320

Length Overall—88 feet 10 inches
Width Overall—10 feet 7 inches
Height Overall—15 feet
Weight on Drivers—405,600 pounds
Total Engine Weight—545,600 pounds
Driving Wheel Diameter—47¼ inches
Guiding Wheel Diameter—37⅜ inches
Gear Ratio—381

Brake Equipment 8-EL
Trucks—General Steel Castings
Motors—Eight GE 750
Control—P
Horsepower—5,120 h.p.
Tractive Effort—77,000 pounds
Maximum Speed—68 m.p.h.

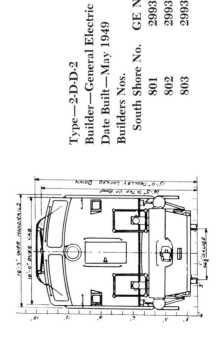

NO SCALE

Freshly rebuilt for South Shore service by the railway's Michigan City shops, "Little Joe" No. 803 headed a November 6, 1949, excursion of the Central Electric Railfans' Assn. that included an extra caboose and a trail coach in the consist of a regular freight. In the head on view at the right, No. 803 is shown at Gary, Indiana.—MWEH COLLECTION (BELOW) The unusual special is shown here running eastbound on the main line just east of the railway's Michigan City shops.—WILLIAM C. JANSSEN

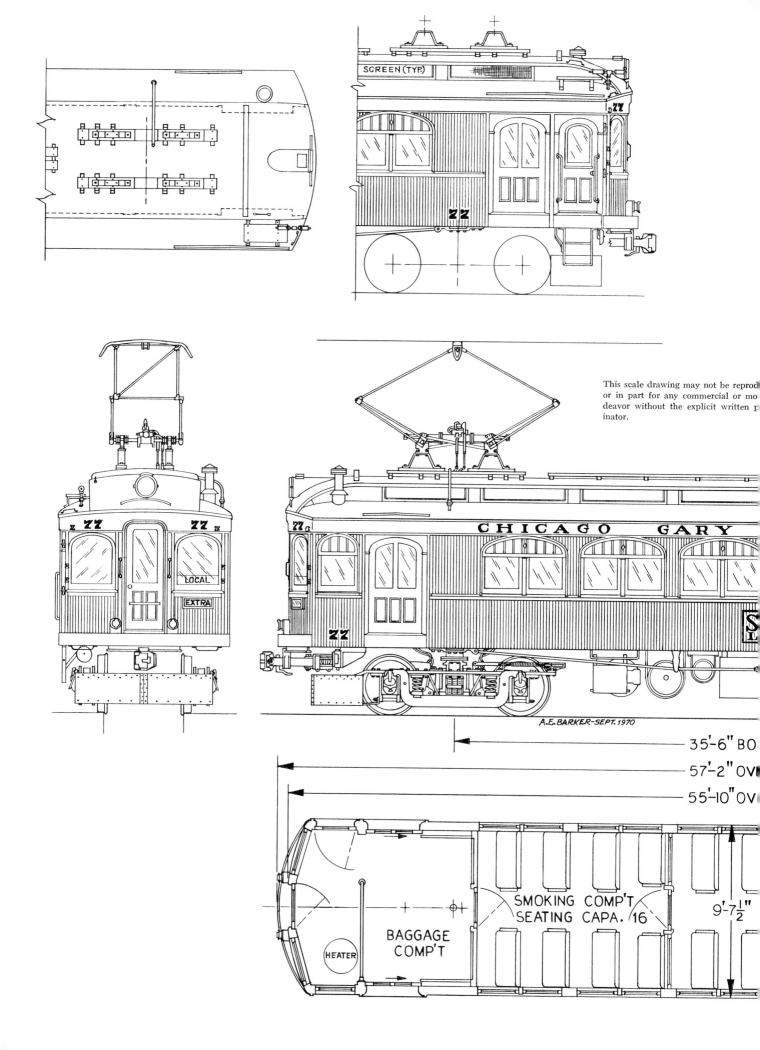

SCREEN (TYP.)

77

77

This scale drawing may not be reprod
or in part for any commercial or mo
deavor without the explicit written p
inator.

LOCAL

EXTRA

77 77

CHICAGO GARY

77

S

A.E. BARKER-SEPT. 1970

35'-6" BO

57'-2" OV

55'-10" OV

9'-7½"

SMOKING COMP'T
SEATING CAPA. 16

BAGGAGE
COMP'T

HEATER

CHICAGO, LAKE SHORE & SOUTH BEND RAILWAY
NO. 75-77

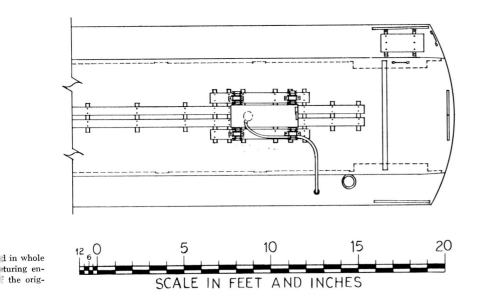

d in whole
turing en-
the orig-

12 0   5   10   15   20
SCALE IN FEET AND INCHES

SPECIFICATIONS AND DATA

Type—Multiple Unit Combine
Builder—Niles Car & Manufacturing Co.
Date Built—1908
Length Overall—57 feet 2 inches
Width Overall—9 feet 10 inches
Height Overall—13 feet 8 inches
Total Weight—111,350 pounds
Wheel Diameter—38 inches
Trucks—Baldwin 90-35
Motors—Four Westinghouse 148-D A.C.
Control—WH-AB
Horsepower—125 h.p.
Maximum Speed—65 m.p.h. on tangent track
Seats—54

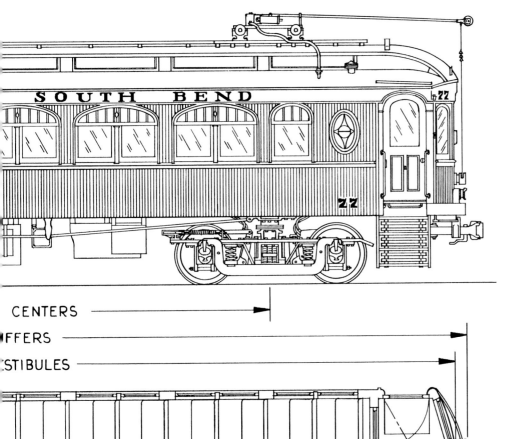

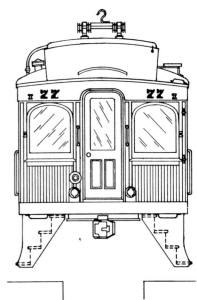

CENTERS

FFERS

STIBULES

MAIN PASSENGER COMPARTMENT
SEATING CAPACITY 38

SCALE—3/16 inch to the foot

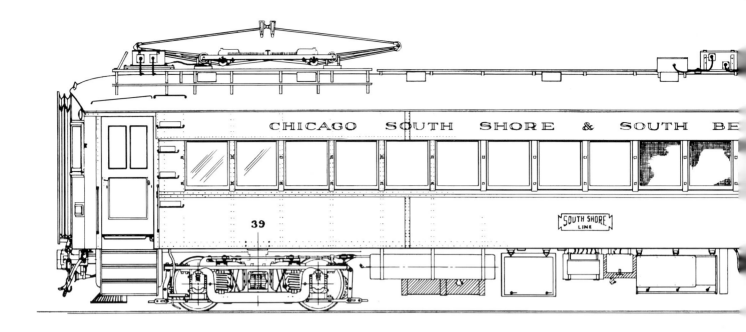

SOUTH SHORE COACH NOS. 30-40

SPECIFICATIONS
AND DATA

Type—Multiple Unit Coach
Builder—Standard Steel Car
Date Built—1929
Length Overall—61 feet
Width Overall—10 feet 1¼ inches
Height Overall—13 feet 4½ inches
Weight on Drivers—129,600 pounds
Total Weight—133,600 pounds
Wheel Diameter—36 inches
Gear Ratio—59/24
Brake Equipment—Westinghouse A.M.U.
Trucks—Baldwin 84-60AA
Motors—Four Westinghouse 567-C11
Control—HBF

Horsepower—210 h.p. per motor
Maximum Speed—75 m.p.h. on tangent track
Seats—48

South Shore's standard cars of the Insull era were among the heaviest and most powerful interurban equipment ever built. In the view above, Standard Steel Car-built (1929) coach No. 30 heads a four-car train at Beverly Shores, Indiana, in 1941.—CHARLES D. SAVAGE (LEFT) In a classic equipment view we find combine No. 100, built by Pullman in 1926.—DONALD DUKE COLLECTION

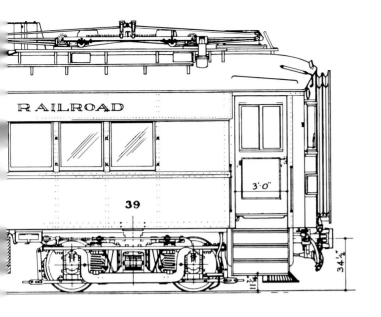

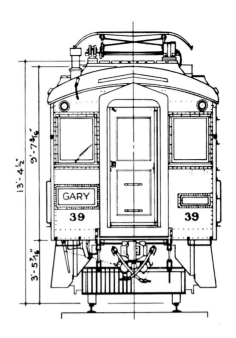

SCALE—3/16 inch to the foot

SOUTH SHORE COMBINE NOS. 100-109

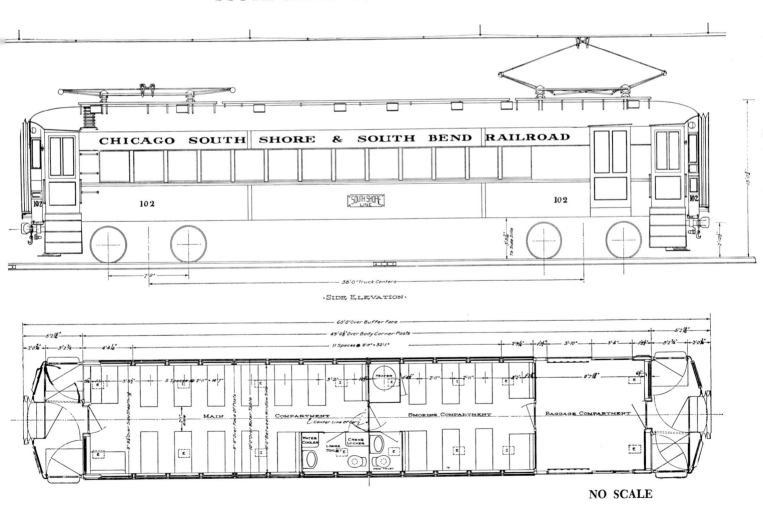

·SIDE ELEVATION·

NO SCALE

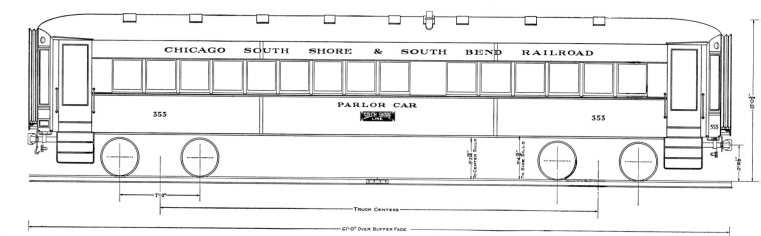

CHICAGO SOUTH SHORE & SOUTH BEND RAILROAD

PARLOR CAR

SOUTH SHORE LINE

353   353

SOUTH SHORE
PARLOR CAR NOS. 353-354

As built by Standard Steel Car in 1929, parlor car
No. 353 seated 24 in plush arm chairs. The luxury
trade soon vanished and a decade later South Shore
rebuilt the car into a 56-seat coach.

(NEXT PAGE) A new generation of South Shore passenger equipment
arrived with the 1982-83 delivery of a new 44-car fleet of 85-foot air-
conditioned, stainless-steel cars built by Japan's Nippon Sharyo. This drawing by David L. Waddington shows one of the initial order. Another 17
nearly identical cars followed from the same builder during 1992–93, while
a third order for another eight to ten cars was pending at the end of 1998.

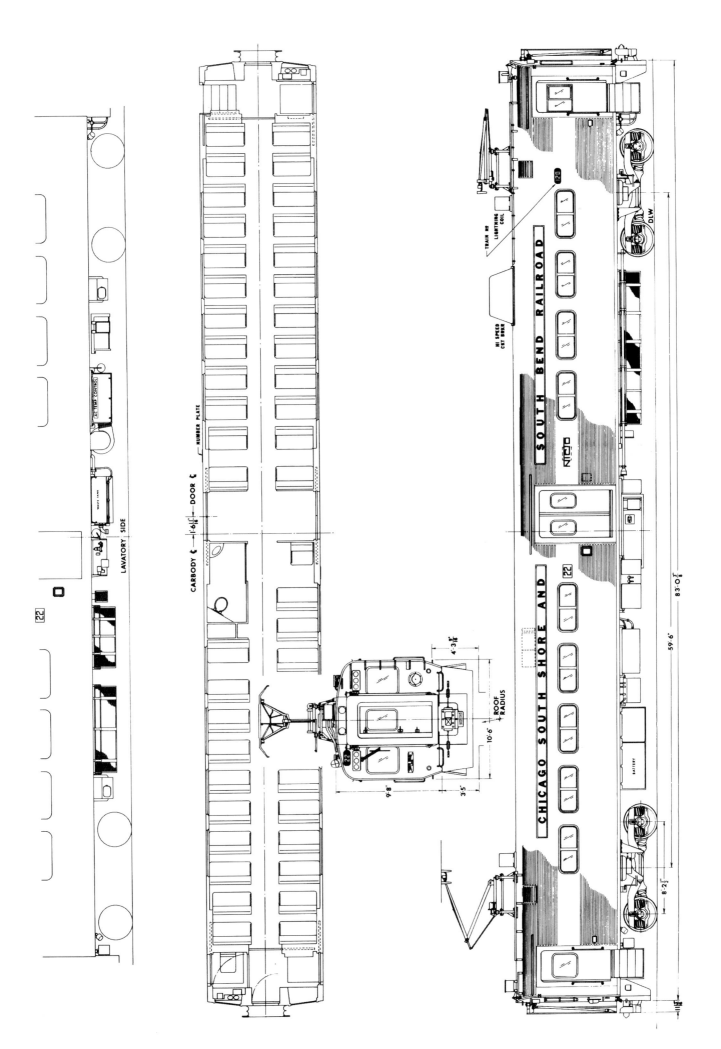

Bibliography

"Art Prize Goes to South Shore Line," *Electric Railway Journal*, Vol. 70, No. 6 (Aug. 6, 1927), page 246.

Birch, L.W., "High Current Capacity with Exceptional Flexibility Feature of Catenary," *Electric Railway Journal*, Vol. 68, No. 22 (Nov. 27, 1926), pages 965–967.

"Building Freight Business," *Electric Traction*, Vol. 24, No. 12 (Dec. 1928), page 621.

Carlson, Norman, Editor, *Chicago South Shore & South Bend Railroad: How the Medal Was Won*. Chicago, Central Electric Railfans' Association, Bulletin No. 124, 1985.

"The Chicago, Lake Shore & South Bend Railway," *Electric Railway Journal*, Vol. 33, No. 15 (April 10, 1909), pages 674–683.

Chicago South Shore & South Bend Railroad. Chicago, Central Electric Railfans' Association, Bulletin No. 4, 1939.

"Coffin Award Won by South Shore Line," *Electric Railway Journal*, Vol. 73, No. 20 (Oct. 1929), pages 975–976.

"Development of Freight Traffic," *Electric Traction*, Vol. 17, No. 6 (June 1921), pages 380–381.

Electric Railways of Indiana. Chicago, Central Electric Railfans' Association, Bulletin No. 104, 1960.

First and Fastest. Michigan City, Ind., Chicago South Shore & South Bend Railroad, 1929.

"Freight Handling by South Shore Lines," *Electric Traction*, Vol. 12, No. 11 (Nov. 1916), pages 866–867.

"Freight Handling on the South Shore Lines," *Electric Traction*, Vol. 14, No. 6 (June 1918), pages 317–321.

"Freight Locomotives for the South Shore Lines," *Electric Railway Journal*, Vol. 48, No. 20 (Nov. 11, 1916), pages 1018–1021.

"'Golden Arrow' between Chicago and Detroit," *Electric Railway Journal*, Vol. 70, No. 6 (Aug. 6, 1927), page 247.

"Good Service Has Paid on the South Shore Line," *Electric Railway Journal*, Vol. 70, No. 20 (Nov. 12, 1927), pages 901–906.

Ingles, J. David, "The Venango River Boys and Their Electric Train," *Trains*, Vol. 45, No. 9 (July 1985), pages 16–17.

Jones, Charles H., "Heavy Interurban Meets the Urge of Automobile Competition," *Electric Railway Journal*, Vol. 70, No. 12 (Sept. 17, 1927), pages 496–498.

———, "The Rehabilitation of the Chicago South Shore & South Bend Railroad," *Baldwin Locomotives*, Vol. 8, No. 1 (July 1929), pages 55–62.

Kaplan, Donald R., *Duneland Electric*. Homewood, Illinois, PTJ Publishing, 1984.

Marlette, Jerry, *Electric Railroads of Indiana*. Indianapolis, Council for Local History, 1959.

Middleton, William D., " . . . and Then There Was One," *Trains*, Vol. 25, No. 4 (Feb. 1965), pages 44–51.

———, "New Cars for the South Shore . . . Finally," *Trains*, Vol. 42, No. 3 (Jan. 1982), pages 48–50.

———, "South Shore's Steel Standards," *Trains*, Vol. 32, No. 10 (Aug. 1972), pages 26–28.

Modernization of Car 15 by the Chicago South Shore & South

Bend Railroad. Chicago, Central Electric Railfans' Association, Bulletin No. 41, September 1942.

"New Ideas in Bus and Rail Stations," *Electric Traction*, Vol. 23, No. 6 (June 1927), pages 330–332.

"New South Shore Equipment in Service," *Electric Railway Journal*, Vol. 68, No. 3 (July 17, 1926), page 123.

"No Traffic Congestion on Steel Highways," *Electric Traction*, Vol. 25, No. 8 (Aug. 1929), pages 399–400.

"Power Station of the Chicago, Lake Shore & South Bend Railway," *Electric Railway Journal*, Vol. 33, No. 16 (Apr. 17, 1909), pages 724–729.

"Recent Equipment Orders," *Electric Traction*, Vol. 24, No. 12 (Dec. 1928), page 646.

"Rehabilitation Brings Results on the South Shore Line," *Electric Railway Journal*, Vol. 70, No. 20 (Nov. 5, 1927), pages 852–856.

Robbins, Dr. John C., "The South Shore: Emergence from Crisis," paper presented at the APTA 1983 Rapid Transit Conference, Pittsburgh, Pa.

"Seven Years of Operating Experience of a Single-Phase Interurban Railway," *Electric Railway Journal*, Vol. 46, No. 19 (Nov. 6, 1915), pages 940–945.

Smerk, George M., Jr., "The Northern Indiana Commuter Transportation District: A Tenth Anniversary Report," *Indiana Business Review*, Vol. 62, No. 4 (Oct. 1987), pages 2–8.

———, "Progress on the South Shore," *Indiana Business Review*, Vol. 59 (March-April 1984), pages 2–7.

———, "The South Shore Makes a Comeback," *CATS Research News*, Vol. 24, No. 1 (March 1985), pages 37–43.

———, "South Shore Update," *Indiana Business Review*, Vol. 57 (February 1982), pages 2, 4–8.

"Shore Line Starts New Service," *Electric Traction*, Vol. 23, No. 8 (Aug. 1927), page 445.

"South Shore Advertises SPEED to Win Riders," *Electric Traction*, Vol. 26, No. 2 (Feb. 1930), pages 60–61.

"South Shore Completes the 'Latest' in Car Shops," *Electric Traction*, Vol. 27, No. 3 (Mar. 1931), pages 109–112.

"The 'South Shore' Could Run Forty-Car Freight Trains," *Electric Railway Journal*, Vol. 51, No. 19 (May 11, 1918), page 906.

"South Shore Interurban Being Improved," *Electric Railway Journal*, Vol. 66, No. 14 (Oct. 3, 1925), pages 562–563.

"South Shore Line Builds Attractive Freight Service," *Electric Railway Journal*, Vol. 71, No. 17 (Apr. 28, 1928), pages 693–695.

"South Shore Line Rehabilitated," *Electric Railway Journal*, Vol. 70, No. 6 (Aug. 6, 1927), pages 218–220.

"South Shore Lines Made New," *Electric Traction*, Vol. 21, No. 12 (Dec. 1925), pages 633–636.

"South Shore Line Starts Dining and Parlor Car Service," *Electric Railway Journal*, Vol. 69, No. 10 (Mar. 5, 1927), pages 417–418.

"South Shore Modernizes Old Cars," *Electric Traction*, Vol. 23, No. 1 (Jan. 1927), pages 25–26.

"South Shore Poster Wins Medals," *Electric Traction*, Vol. 23, No. 7 (July 1927), page 354.

"South Shore Starts Big Improvement Program," *Electric Railway Journal*, Vol. 69, No. 5 (Jan. 29, 1927), page 228.

"South Shore Starts New Service," *Electric Traction*, Vol. 22, No. 8 (Aug. 1926), pages 392–393.

"South Shore Wins Coffin Medal," *Electric Traction*, Vol. 25, No. 10 (Oct. 1929), page 517.

Spangler, L.A., "Hauling Holiday Crowds on the South Shore Line," *Electric Traction*, Vol. 19, No. 3 (Mar. 1923), pages 110–111.

"Specifications on Cars for South Shore Line," *Electric Railway Journal*, Vol. 72, No. 24 (Dec. 15, 1928), page 1065.

"Speed with Spring Switches," *Electric Traction*, Vol. 24, No. 12 (Dec. 1928), pages 629–630.

"Successor Company to South Shore Takes Charge," *Electric Railway Journal*, Vol. 66, No. 3 (July 18, 1925), page 109.

"Ten Units Being Built for South Shore Line," *Electric Railway Journal*, Vol. 72, No. 2 (July 14, 1928), page 81.

The Transportation Corridor in Northwest Indiana. Bloomington and Indianapolis, The Institute for Urban Transportation, School of Business, Indiana University, 1978.

"Twenty New Steel Motors and Trailers for the South Shore Line," *Electric Railway Journal*, Vol. 70, No. 14 (Oct. 1, 1927), page 617.

Wilby, N.H., "Control on New South Shore Cars," *Electric Traction*, Vol. 22, No. 12 (Dec. 1926), pages 653–654.

Wilcoxon, C.N., "Operation of Single-Phase Interurban," *Electric Traction*, Vol. 18, No. 6 (June 1922), pages 489–492.

Index

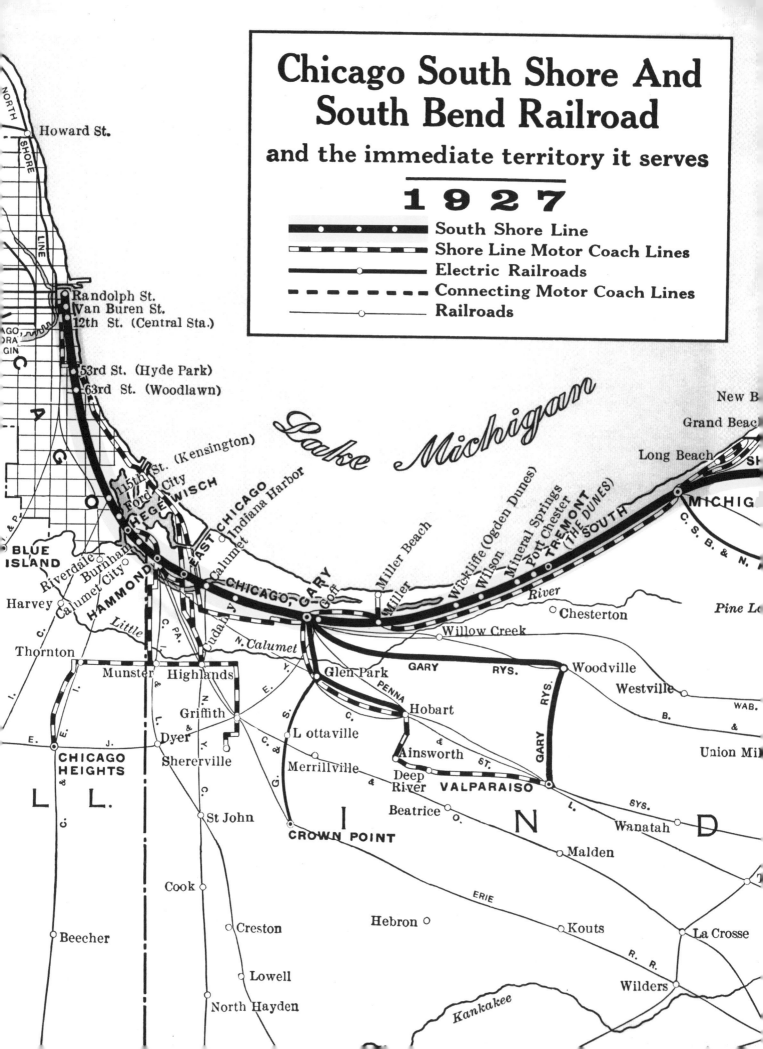